The Whitworth Art Gallery

The First Hundred Years

British Gas plc
The Committee of the Whitworth Art Gallery
and its Director, Professor C R Dodwell,
record their appreciation to British Gas plc and
British Gas North Western whose financial
assistance has made it possible
to publish this Centenary guide.

Foreword

We publish this latest illustrated guide to the Whitworth Art Gallery, made possible by a generous subvention from British Gas plc, to mark the centenary of the Gallery's foundation in 1889. It is the first guide to be illustrated in colour and it highlights some of the most outstanding works acquired in our first hundred years. It includes items from the departments of Paintings, Drawings and Sculpture, Prints, Textiles and Wallpapers, arranged in broadly chronological order.

The individual entries on the works of art have been written by the curators responsible for their care, namely, Joanna Banham, former Research Assistant, Wallpapers, Jennifer Harris, Assistant Keeper, Textiles, Sarah Hyde, Assistant Keeper, Prints, Francis Hawcroft, Principal Keeper, Greg Smith, Assistant Keeper, Art and Christine Woods, Research Assistant, Wallpapers. The design and production of the guide was overseen by Julian Tomlin, Exhibitions Officer and Peter Burton and Michael Pollard have taken the photographs. To all of them I extend my thanks.

The guide was designed by the Whitworth Art Gallery and Barron Hatchett, Manchester and I am most grateful to Neville Stott. The printing was undertaken by Stanley Press, Dewsbury where Graham Seed in particular has been most helpful.

Since I have edited the whole, and rewritten parts, I must accept responsibility for any inaccuracies that remain.

C.R. Dodwell **Director**

September 1988

Contents

The Whitworth Art Gallery
The First Hundred Years

There is a certain curiosity about the circumstances surrounding the foundation of the Whitworth Art Gallery.

We might, I suppose, expect the founder of a university gallery to be drawn from the aristocracy like Fitzwilliam at Cambridge, or at least the higher ranks of the professional classes like Ashmole at Oxford. But Whitworth came from neither. We would certainly expect such a founder to be a scholar. Yet in terms of higher academic training Whitworth was uneducated. It is quite certain that, as a technologist, he was highly talented but, although he did own some nineteenth-century paintings by Royal Academicians, he never seemed particularly interested in art. The Whitworth Art Gallery was in fact a posthumous child that he never saw or even imagined.

Sir Joseph Whitworth—as he was later to become—was born in 1803 at Stockport near Manchester. He came of comparatively humble stock, being the son of a local schoolmaster. At the age of 14, he was apprenticed for four years to his uncle who was a cotton spinner in Derbyshire, and there he quickly showed his immense aptitude for things mechanical and soon mastered the working of every machine in the factory. He decided to become an engineer, and in 1821 went to the machine-making shop of Messrs. Chrighton and Company in Manchester. In afterlife, he said that the happiest day in his life was when he first earned a journeyman's wage there. In 1826, he married his first wife and soon after moved to London to Messrs. Maudslay, and it was whilst there that he developed a technique for the preparation of perfect plane surfaces.

Fig 1 **Sir Joseph Whitworth**
portrait by T.B. Kennington after L. Desanges

Later, he was to perpetuate his name by establishing a uniform and internationally recognised standard for screw-threads that was accepted everywhere until very recently. When he moved back to Manchester he founded a business that was to become world-famous. He himself achieved public eminence at the Great Exhibition in London of 1851 where he exhibited a collection of engineers' tools, and again at the Paris Exhibition of 1867 where he was awarded one of the prizes. He was honoured by the Universities of Oxford and Dublin with honorary degrees; in 1868 he received the Legion of Honour from Napoleon III; in 1869 he was made a baronet. In 1871, after the death of his first wife in the intervening year, he married again. His main leisure-time activity in later years was that of gardening, and he devoted much of his time to laying out the grounds of his estate at Stancliffe, near Macclesfield. His Manchester residence was *The Firs* at Fallowfield where the Vice-Chancellors of the University of Manchester now live, though at the end of his life he took to wintering on the Riviera and it was at Monte Carlo that he died in January 1887 at the age of 84.

By hard work, inventiveness and care for detail he had amassed a large fortune. And, since he was so scrupulous about detail himself, we might record that the exact figure was £1,227,781 9s 1d.

We have a portrait of Whitworth at the entrance to the Gallery *(figure 1)* in which he looks more appealing than he did to Mrs Carlyle who visited Manchester in 1846 and from there wrote to her husband the following account

Fig 2 **Robert Dukinfield Darbishire** portrait by T.B. Kennington

of this area:

> *There is no lack of interesting people here and they have a great superiority over the London people, for every man here knows what he is about and is able and willing to give a straightforward account of it. Whitworth, the inventor of... many... wonderful machines, has a face not unlike a baboon; speaks the broadest Lancashire; could not invent an epigram to save his life; but has nevertheless a talent which might drive the genii to despair and when one talks with him, one feels that one is talking with a real live man, to my mind worth any number of the wits that go about.*

A more friendly and perhaps more accurate account of Whitworth was given by his friend Darbishire, who said of him that "his character was that of a man of the simplest and healthiest taste, characterised by what has been described as the pure mark of genius, an infinite capacity for taking pains and an infallible determination to think and do only what appeared to him to be right".

Whitworth, as we have seen, left on his death a vast fortune of more than a million pounds. But the very qualities that had led to the amassing of the fortune made the disposal of it very tortuous, for we are told that Whitworth's "passionate desire of extreme accuracy in every detail... perpetually interfered with any absolute settlement of his plans". Eventually, however, the bulk of it was left to three residuary legatees (one of them his wife) with instructions that it should be used for charitable and educational purposes. Around £416,000, for example, went to found Engineering Scholarships, and about £157,000 was initially set on one side to form a Whitworth Institute which was originally intended to have a School of Technology and a School of Art integrated with an Art Gallery. In the event, the Schools of Technology and of Art, together with money for an endowment, were taken over by the City Council.

Here, I think, it should be stressed that the initiative for the Gallery itself lay largely in the hands of Whitworth's friend who was one of his residuary legatees. He was Robert Dukinfield Darbishire, whom we have mentioned above and whose portrait, appropriately enough, hangs opposite that of Whitworth in our entrance hall (*figure 2*). He, more than anyone else, was the real founder of the Gallery. I have spoken of Whitworth as being a rather unlikely founder of an art gallery. In fact, if we look at the historical facts, we shall probably agree that Whitworth himself was less the father of the enterprise than its father-in-law. He provided the dowry which Darbishire applied with taste and discrimination.

Darbishire and the other two residuary legatees began by assembling a group of eminent Mancunians to form

2

Fig 3 **Grove House** 1904

a committee. Amongst them were C.P. Scott, the editor of the *Manchester Guardian,* and others from families with which we still have associations. These included William (later Sir William) Mather M.P., and William (later Sir William) Agnew of the famous firm of art-dealers of that name which then had an outlet in Manchester. The very first picture given to the Institute was, in fact, an oil painting by G.F. Watts called *Love and Death* (p.92) which was presented by the artist through the good offices of Sir William Agnew.

The Committee of the projected Institute got down to work very quickly and bought Whitworth Park, which was then known as Potter's Field. They were determined in their own words to establish a

worthy memorial of our late friend... which shall secure at once a source of perpetual gratification to the people of Manchester and, at the same time, a permanent influence of the highest character in the directions of Commercial and Technical Instruction and the cultivation of taste and knowledge of the Fine Arts of Painting, Sculpture and Architecture.

The charter of the envisaged Institute was sealed on October 2nd 1889, and under its terms sixty distinguished Manchester citizens were appointed Governors of the Institute (between fifty and a hundred were allowed by the Royal Charter) with power to elect an Executive Council. They used Grove House in Whitworth Park for exhibitions, and in *figure 4* we show a photograph of such an exhibition with the two textiles, *Flora* and *Pomona,* (which we shall come to later) already displayed on the left-hand wall. It was a house that, according to a statement made by Lady Alice Bragg in 1966, had hitherto been the home of the Hopkinson family with their thirteen children and an Alderney cow! A competition to find the best architect for the Gallery was set up and assessed by Alfred Waterhouse, and it was won by J.W. and J. Beaumont. They began the new building on a site to the west of Grove House, which was itself finally demolished to make way for the front part of the Gallery as we know it today, and *figure 3* shows the east front of the house with the roof of the present South Gallery just behind it to the left. Their activities proceeded in two stages: the

Fig 4 **Grove House, Corridor Gallery**

first was begun in 1895 and completed in 1897, and the second was completed in 1908. The new building was to include not only rooms for hanging pictures but also areas for lectures and concerts and, though the inside of the Gallery was to change, its outside, faced with red Ruabon brick and given a somewhat romantic appearance by its towers and turrets, looks exactly now as it did then.

These were happy days for the Whitworth, and when the completed gallery was opened in 1908 by the Director of the National Gallery, Sir Charles Holroyd, he used a couplet of Stevenson as his theme:

> *The world is full of a number of things*
> *I am sure we all ought to be as happy as kings.*

The *Manchester Guardian* echoed the optimistic strain and described the Whitworth as "one of the most interesting and promising art galleries of the country". It "is already interesting", it said a little sententiously, and "may yet be famous." In fact its fame was later to rest on collections which had been largely initiated in the earliest days by the interests of particular Governors.

We have seen that one of the original ideas for the

Fig 5 **North West Gallery** 1905-6

Gallery was that it should not only cultivate taste and knowledge in the Fine Arts but also offer instruction, and this would account for the way in which early acquisitions consisted of so many copies. Not least of these were casts of classical sculpture (later distributed to schools in the early 1920s), and we illustrate in *figure 5* a photograph of how these casts were displayed in the Gallery around 1906 (in *figure 4*, we saw how they were exhibited in Grove House). Initial ideas about the rôle of the Gallery would also account for the very miscellaneous character of the early objects, which included a marble head of Medusa by G.F. Watts, a large painting by him of *Love and Death* already referred to (p.92), a Japanese bronze trophy embellished with plant forms, elephants and mice which cost no less than £4,000, and a cotton handkerchief with a print of Peterloo. But galleries, like children, do not always grow into the rôles their parents have fondly imagined for them and this one very quickly showed unexpected personality traits which were to bring it to later eminence.

Probably the most famed amongst our present collections is our English watercolours. It is certainly one of the finest in the world and was initiated by the interest of two of the first Governors. One was William (later Sir William) Agnew who was chairman of the Guarantors of the Manchester Royal Jubilee exhibition, and these Guarantors gave just under £42,000 to the Whitworth thus helping to finance the purchase of some forty watercolours. The other was the Director of the *Manchester Guardian*, John Edward Taylor, who in 1893 gave a choice selection of 154 English watercolours from his own fine collection, all carefully chosen to illustrate the history of the watercolour tradition. John Taylor's generous benefaction was as remarkable in quality as it was in quantity, and it included some of our best known drawings: William Blake's *Ancient of Days* (p.66), John Robert Cozens' *The Lake of Nemi* (p.58), Thomas Girtin's *Durham Cathedral and Bridge* (p.60), Turner's *Fire at Fenning's Wharf*, and so on. This benefaction, together with the early purchases, formed the nucleus of a collection of English watercolours which today can only be paralleled in the Victoria and Albert Museum and the British Museum, and which has been strengthened throughout the history of the Gallery by important gifts. We reproduce in *figure 12* a photograph of a display of the Whitworth's watercolours in the South Gallery in 1898, which demonstrates both the early recognition of their importance and the display methods fashionable at the time. (It is a fashion that can still be seen in the print rooms of one or two English country houses, like The Vyne in Hampshire, a fashion that even the modern eye can quickly adapt to.)

Our collection of historic textiles is also of tremendous significance—it is second only to that in the Victoria and Albert Museum—and its initiation was due to careful forethought and deliberation.

Among the original intentions of the Governors was the formation of a collection of textiles to act as a source of help and inspiration for the textile industry of the North. Already in 1888, those beautiful and refreshing tapestries designed by William Morris and Edward Burne-Jones, *Flora* (p.86) and *Pomona*, had been bought for the anticipated new Institute, and in 1891 the great collection of early textiles and embroidery that had been assembled by Sir Charles Robinson was purchased. He, anxious to help his friends on the Whitworth Council, parted with it for a nominal sum. They included some ravishing Italian silk damasks and velvets of the sixteenth and seventeenth centuries, and some lovely Italian and French silk brocades and satins of the seventeenth to the nineteenth. The collection also contained a number of ecclesiastical vestments, most particularly, gorgeous Spanish ones of the sixteenth and seventeenth centuries embroidered with gold, delicious vestments of satin to be used in festivals, and a sombre black velvet cope with skulls and crossed bones in white silk appliqué for use on Good Friday and for general mourning (p.24). We know from a letter written by Sir Charles Robinson that it was with particular reluctance that he parted with a fine fifteenth-century German woven altar-frontal (p.18) which represents a

medieval theme, that of the Tree of Jesse, and which remains one of the treasures of our collection as it was of his. Before very long, this great collection was supplemented by accessions of Egyptian and Coptic textiles which also derived from Sir Charles, and which were associated in a general way with the famous Egyptian excavator Professor Sir William Flinders Petrie. These Mediterranean textiles—so important for an understanding of medieval themes—ranged from the fourth century A.D. to the eleventh, and included some fine examples and even one or two complete robes. Our holdings in this area were yet further enriched when the Manchester Museum transferred its fine collection of Coptic textiles to us in 1968 on permanent loan (see p.16).

On the basis of these collections, the Gallery has built its present formidable holdings of textiles, and though we have never made good our weakness in the centuries of the medieval West, we are rich in most other periods of western history. With the support of important gifts such as that from Professor and Mrs P.E. Newberry in 1949, we have also continued to expand our Oriental holdings which now cover China, Japan, India (see p.40), Persia (see p.26), Turkey and Iran (see p.90). We also continually enlarge our contemporary collections, and, in this, we have been helped by the generosity of Warner and Sons Ltd., and Designers' Guild and Collier Campbell Ltd.

The third of our really important collections—that of prints—was anticipated from quite early on, for in 1906 the Gallery bought from the Earl of Westmorland, for a nominal consideration, seventy-two prints of Turner's *Liber Studiorum* which formed "a singularly complete series in the finest condition". However, our real strengths result from later substantial acquisitions and chiefly relate to periods of the Renaissance. I am particularly thinking of the great acquisition in 1921 of Mr G.T. Clough's valuable collection of German and Italian woodcuts and engravings of the fifteenth and sixteenth centuries, to the formation of which Mr Clough had devoted much time and exacting scholarship. It included examples of the work of masters like Dürer (see p.22), Mantegna, Pollaiuolo and Rembrandt. This collection was considerably enlarged and enhanced in 1926 by Mr W. Sharp Ogden's generous bequest of his fine collection of Old Master prints of a different period. Since then, our print collection has been extended by many generous gifts from donors like Mr Denis F. Pilkington, and was further enriched when the History of Art Department of the University handed over its own collections, which included one of about 300 Japanese prints to join other examples of this exquisite art in the Gallery. Private benefactions of particular note were made by Dr Percy Withers, Mr Joseph Knight, Mrs Max Meyer and Mrs O. Beer.

A fourth collection, that of historic wallpapers, is second in importance only to that in the Victoria and Albert Museum and we owe it, much as it is today, to the great generosity of the Wall Paper Manufacturers Ltd. whose representatives, after discussions with the Director, offered it to the Gallery in 1967. It was, of course, most gladly accepted.

This collection, which contains pieces of the very highest quality going back to the seventeenth century, was founded by Alan V. Sugden who was a Chairman of the firm for 25 years and who was also joint-author of *A History of English Wallpaper 1509-1914*. He was determined to produce a definitive history of the industry, and to this end both built up this superb collection and researched the field in person and with others. One Director of the firm, Eric Entwisle, who was particularly interested in assisting with the research, continued to build up the collection after Mr Sugden's retirement in 1948, and to him and to Edward Pond and Robert Grime, we are indebted for the idea of transferring the collection to the Gallery. A home in the North-West seemed to me at the time a particularly appropriate one since this was the traditional base for the machine printing of wallpapers (it was pioneered by Potters of Darwen in 1841), and these holdings also tied in very neatly with others in our Departments of Prints and Textiles. An exhibition, drawn from the donated wallpapers, was shown in the Gallery in 1972 and was very well received.

The cataloguing of this vast collection called for special arrangements but it was not until 1983 that money could be found for this. The British Academy generously responded to the Director's request for funds to finance an expert cataloguer for three years, and there was additional help from the Pilgrim Trust. When this period was completed, the Greater Manchester Council agreed to finance a more permanent appointment, and with further help from them, and generous help from the North West Museum and Gallery Service, we were able to set up a properly equipped Wallpapers Room for a new Department which has since become a particularly active one. More recently, the Manchester-based manufacturer of wallpapers, Coloroll Ltd., has made donations to the Department, thus confirming the particular relevance of this collection to the North-West of England.

Today, most of our collection is the one presented in 1967, though it has been supplemented by much appreciated gifts from Crown Wallcoverings Ltd. and Edward Bawden, and we have also begun making important purchases of our own.

Our fifth Department, of modern and contemporary art, might almost be called our first in so far as the very first painting acquired by the original Whitworth Institute was a contemporary one, Watts' *Love and Death* (p.92), which we have mentioned above. Then, in 1888, even before the charter for the new Institute had been signed and sealed, the contemporary tapestries of *Flora* and *Pomona* by Morris and Burne-Jones (p.86) had been bought in anticipation of the new Gallery's inauguration (we have earlier seen that they were exhibited in Grove House). In fact, the Whitworth has continued to acquire contemporary works from its very beginning and, as a result, I do not have sufficient space here to survey its collections of modern and contemporary art in historical terms, since this would involve a detailed examination of such acquisitions at each phase of the Gallery's development. I shall therefore have to content myself by remarking that, since becoming a university gallery, we have pursued a deliberate policy of buying works of art by contemporary British artists, and our collection as a result now contains works by artists of the calibre of Henry Moore, Barbara Hepworth, Hockney, Bacon, Freud and so on. In all of this I would like to express the Gallery's warm appreciation of the generous financial help given by the Friends of the Whitworth Art Gallery and the National Art-Collections Fund. This modern and contemporary collection was much enhanced in 1987 by a substantial bequest from Hal Burton of his own choice pictures which included a delightful Matthew Smith and fine works by Henry Moore, John Piper, Graham Sutherland, Rex Whistler, Paul Nash, Augustus John, and so on.

Seeds of future greatness were mostly sown in its early

Fig 6 **Whitworth Park** before 1904

days, and then the Gallery was part of a much broader plan, for the founders had ideas which were admirably wide-ranging. They set aside parts of the Gallery for concerts and lectures, and at very considerable expense they also drained and laid out Whitworth Park as a pleasure garden. It had its own band-stand and a large lake for sailing, and the Governors sent the park super-

intendent as far afield as Brussels to get ideas for its development. Our illustration in *figure 6* presents a view of the boating lake and pavilion before 1904. This pleasure garden meant much to the main Committee, and the Minutes of their earliest meetings make a number of references to it commenting, for example, on how much it was used by visitors and children "of all classes" and how often concerts were given.

These appeared to be halcyon days for the Whitworth. Yet, there were some cracks in the foundation and these were financial ones. It would seem that they derived from three principal causes—the first that the anticipated financial support from the City of Manchester had not been forthcoming: the second that the original capital sum available had been considerably reduced by endowments handed over to the Schools of Art and Technology: and the third (though, to my mind, the first in importance) that so much money was spent on the park. This cost nearly £70,000 to purchase and lay out at a time when it was envisaged that £36,000 would be sufficient to endow the Gallery itself, though a further £50,000 was added for the Gallery in 1893 when the legatees had to face up to the financial realities of a new building. Further to all this, the original appraisal of the running costs of a large park and Gallery was over-optimistic and, in the event, the Governors decided quite soon to hand the park over to the City since they could not afford the annual expenses involved: it was a park that had cost the Governors almost half the sum originally set aside for the Institute as a whole. Yet, in this context, we should emphasise that the main concern of the legatees and Governors had always been to provide a memorial for Whitworth, and this extensive green park within the inner area of a major city did, and still does, much to keep his name alive. In October 1904, the park was formally handed over on a thousand year lease for a nominal rent of £10 a year. After lunching at the Town Hall, members of the City Council came down by electric car to Whitworth Park, and the Mayor in his chain of office took over the park to the

7

Fig 7 **Margaret Pilkington** portrait by Sir Stanley Spencer 1953

the Institute has caused serious concern to the Council... The Council therefore point out that it is urgent that the endowment of the Institute should be augmented to cover at least its present annual deficits". As one looks through the records, one sees a gradual deterioration of the financial situation in the early part of this century as the investments of the Gallery depreciated.

The decline was halted for a short period by the First World War when the building was requisitioned (this in 1917) and it was not returned to its original use until September 1920. Some limited compensation was paid by the Government, but the war had driven up wages and costs and the investments of the Gallery, especially its railway stock, continued to slip, so that the financial position of the institution in the inter-war period continued to be much the same as before 1914. Indeed, in 1920, the Governors were even requested to put their hands into their own pockets and contribute towards the running of the place, and this is what these public spirited Mancunians did. Even so, the Minutes of their proceedings begin to read like an accountant's nightmare and, without going into detail, we can see all this reflected in the headlines of the *Manchester Guardian*.

April 1st 1924   *Whitworth Institute's Need*
                        Shortage of Funds curtails work
May 6th 1927   *Whitworth Art Galleries*
                        Further Endowment of £10,000 Needed
March 27th 1930 *Whitworth Art Gallery*
                        Cost of Maintenance
                        Very little to spend on new works
March 27th 1931 *Straitened Finance*
                        Penury at Whitworth Park

In the latter year there was an overdraft of £646. The building had not been redecorated for thirty years, and the Friends of the Whitworth were set up with the particular intention that they should raise money to purchase pictures. It is perhaps little wonder that the

playing of the police band. But, even this action failed to solve the financial problems of the Whitworth Gallery.

In the very following year, a report declared that there was an overdraft of £575, and already in 1908 there were thoughts of an Appeal which thoughts were to recur again in 1920 and 1921. In 1912 there was a deficit of £187, and this led to the statement that "The financial position of

Curator, G.P. Dudley Wallis, had a nervous breakdown about this time.

But happily, there was a benefactress in the wings. Miss Margaret Pilkington stepped in, and in order to save the expenditure of one salary she became Honorary Director of the Whitworth. For over twenty years she gave her services freely to the Gallery, and she and her sister, Dorothy, helped to finance it in many unpublicised ways. An early woman student of the Slade School of Art, a competent artist who numbered many artists among her personal friends, a clear-minded organiser who brought new ideas with her, she was for many years the very life-blood of the Gallery. When, in fact, the Gallery was eventually transferred to the University, one newspaper said that along with it went one of its chief assets, Miss Margaret Pilkington, and there was no-one in Manchester who would not have applauded that remark. We have in the Gallery an arresting drawing of her by Sir Stanley Spencer *(figure 7)*. It makes her look more severe than she did in the flesh but it otherwise catches her appearance and it certainly registers the penetrating glance with which she always met you.

Yet, however gloomy the finances of the Gallery may have been in the inter-war years, its artistic side in the first half of the period was far from that, and it is heartening and remarkable to see how much was happening in the field that the Whitworth served.

Great gifts of works of art were coming in, and they included G.T. Clough's and W. Sharp Ogden's splendid collections of historic prints mentioned earlier, numbers of modern British woodcuts and wood-engravings donated by Margaret Pilkington, and bequests of watercolours made by Mancunians like Sir Edward Tootal Broadhurst. During this time, the Gallery was reorganising and cataloguing some of its collections and also holding important exhibitions: exhibitions, for example, of the drawings of John Robert Cozens and John Sell Cotman, of English embroideries, of Medieval Art, of Old Master Drawings from Holland, and of applied arts from Greece,

Norway and Switzerland. The exhibition of the gifts of Mr A.E. Anderson (from Chessington, Surrey), which was mounted in 1931 was particularly impressive, and one aspect of it is perhaps unique. Over the years, beginning in 1906, he had given to the Gallery hundreds of watercolours and prints by artists, including those of the stature of Cézanne, Degas, Seurat and Girtin, yet he had never once set foot in the Whitworth Gallery or even (it seems) in Manchester. He was invited to this very exhibition and accepted, but at the very last moment he seems to have felt unable to face the warm welcome that was awaiting him and he simply did not turn up; to the best of our knowledge, he never once saw the Gallery that he had enriched so purposefully and over so long a period. We may add that, as well as attracting gifts, the Gallery had made a number of significant, indeed enlightened, purchases of its own, and these had included drawings or watercolours by Impressionists like Degas and Van Gogh, by English artists of the past like Blake, Bonington, Turner, Towne, Gainsborough and Burne-Jones, and by contemporaries like Augustus John, John Nash, Paul Nash and Henry Moore.

All this, however, was confined to the period before 1929. In this year, following proposals already made in 1927 and 1928, the Council decided to utilise the fund originally set aside for the purchase of works of art for general purposes, and they diverted it to help finance repairs to the building. This marked the beginning of the final downwards spiral for, in the 1930s, we find that the Council actually sold their own paintings, prints and watercolours to pay for the general upkeep of the buildings. The Council had, in fact, given consideration to the sale of oil paintings, prints and drawings as far back as 1923, but this was the first time that they felt forced to put this unhappy idea into action.

The Second World War, like the First, brought an interruption to the life of the Gallery, and its best works of art were evacuated. The Whitworth, nevertheless, managed to soldier on for a while, until it was forced to close down in December 1940 after air raids in the area. Its cellars were then used as a reception area for people who had been made homeless by bombing, and it was typical of the public spiritedness of Margaret Pilkington that she personally helped to look after them. After the end of hostilities the life of the Gallery was renewed—but unfortunately not its finances which remained in their depressing pre-war plight—and within a few years, in 1950, the Chairman, Sir Thomas Barlow, was driven to declare:

The balance showed us an undeviating record of gloom. The deficiency would have to be analysed but we had probably reached the depths to which we could sink... if it were not for the voluntary work of Miss Pilkington and the assistance and gifts of some of our supporters, our position would be quite intolerable.

By then, a strange position had arisen. The Whitworth had built up artistic holdings which, by any criterion, were of international importance yet there was insufficient money to keep and maintain the place. The Director was voluntary and honorary. The members of staff, who should have been acting as attendants, were spending part of their time on works of maintenance. And the Governors were continuing, indeed accelerating, the policy of the 1930s of selling off works of art from within the collection to meet current expenditure.

To these financial difficulties the *Manchester Guardian* addressed itself on October 6th 1950, and it declared:

Because of financial difficulties, the Whitworth Art Gallery has for some time been looking for a sponsor... The gallery... has shown a deficit on the balance sheet for a number of years, and though every economy is being made the position continues to get worse.

The newspaper then goes on to say that, in the view of the Governors, the ideal solution would be if the University took it over and it became a parallel organisation to the Fitzwilliam Museum in Cambridge.

In the event, Manchester University *was* approached, and in due course the Gallery *was* transferred to it, though the negotiations ran into numerous legal difficulties since the original Institute had been set up by Royal Charter. They were difficulties which were ultimately resolved by William (later Sir William) Mansfield Cooper who had replaced Sir John Stopford as Vice-Chancellor during the course of the discussions, and who was always keenly interested in the Gallery. Ultimately the Gallery was officially handed over in 1958, and the Earl of Crawford, who presided over the ceremony, put the whole event in its proper perspective. It was, he said, the happiest solution for both parties: the Whitworth would gain security and continuity under its new aegis; the University had gained a great and noble Institute and a new distinction and status for itself. The former body of Governors continued, and Miss Pilkington became the Deputy Chairman. She and her sister endowed a new Chair (known as the Pilkington Chair) of the History of Art in the University, and the first two Professors, like Miss Pilkington before them, were to become Honorary Directors of the Gallery.

The first Professorial Director was John White, who came to the Gallery from the Courtauld Institute in October 1959. He was joined by Francis Hawcroft who, until then, had been in Norwich, and who—appropriately in view of the Gallery's richness in this area—was an expert on watercolours, and later inspired by White to an added interest in contemporary art. Like other curators before 1978, he was appointed to a lectureship in the History of Art Department and paid through that body, and he was made Keeper of the Gallery in 1959 and Principal Keeper in 1978. Francis, as he was referred to by everyone, concentrated much of his interest on the watercolour and contemporary collections, making a number of perceptive purchases for both these areas over the years, and also arranging two or three particularly fine exhibitions of the great English watercolourists. He served

Fig 8 **Darbishire Hall** 1966

Fig 9 **Darbishire Hall** 1968

the Gallery with distinction until his untimely death in 1988 when the number of persons at his Memorial Service in Manchester Cathedral indicated how large was the circle of his friends.

The University set to work on their new acquisition with alacrity and enthusiasm, and quickly made a really major decision, namely to remodel the greater part of the Gallery. It was a decision very much prompted by Sir William Mansfield Cooper, but he was fortunate in having in Professor White a man of vigour and taste who, during the seven years of his appointment, energised the Gallery, revitalised the Friends, and built up a special interest in contemporary art (it was he who initiated the *Northern* (later *Whitworth) Young Contemporaries* exhibitions). The architect that Professor White selected for the new enterprise, John Bickerdike, showed great sensitivity in his recasting of the building. His vision was that of a Gallery retaining its Victorian/Edwardian shell, but completely remodelled within, in accordance with the best contemporary ideas. His conceptions, as they took shape, gave pleasure and delight both to those of the Old Dispensation like Margaret Pilkington and to those of the New like Mansfield Cooper. The measure of Bickerdike's achievement is better seen than described, and, instead of lengthy descriptions at this point, I therefore think it best to reproduce photographs of three of the major areas of the Gallery as they were before and after his architectural transformations. They are: the Darbishire Hall *(figures 8 and 9)*, the North Gallery which was enlarged by Bickerdike with a mezzanine floor *(figures 10 and 11)*, and the South Gallery *(figures 12 and 13)*. (For the latter comparison, I use a photograph of 1898, and not one of the 1940s or 50s, since this enables me to illustrate the display of watercolours of that year.)

The internal rebuilding proceeded in three stages. Stage 1 saw the opening out of the central area of the Gallery and its refinement by a new elegance of design enhanced by the use of natural materials. The exhibition areas were given flexibility by a system of movable display screens and made more comfortable by new heating systems. The first room beyond the entrance hall had always been known as the Darbishire Hall after the man whose energy and foresight had led to the building of the Whitworth, and, with equal appropriateness, the redesigned Central Gallery (now hung with watercolours of the eighteenth and nineteenth centuries) was named after Margaret

Pilkington to whom the continuation of the Gallery had owed so much. A mezzanine floor was added, and the attractive Gulbenkian Room, formed from a corridor and its flanking two rooms, was given this title to commemorate the financial help given by the Gulbenkian Foundation. The first stage of the Gallery reconstruction was opened by Lord Cottesloe, Chairman of the Arts Council, on May 4th 1964, and some two years later in the summer of 1966, Professor White left Manchester for a new post in the U.S.A.

Fig 10 **North Gallery** 1966

He was succeeded by Professor C.R. Dodwell, who came from Trinity College, Cambridge, and who was the Director during the two later stages of the rebuilding. These dealt with the rest of the public display space of the Gallery at ground floor level, and also provided an extension of the mezzanine floor over the North Gallery. In a more pedestrian, but very useful way, these stages of the rebuilding also dealt with the reorganisation of storage space and offices. The most impressive of the redeveloped areas was perhaps the South Gallery, with

its pleasing dimensions and its refreshing views over Whitworth Park—a Park which still belongs to the Gallery even if, in the year of our centenary, it will remain on lease to the City for a further 915 years! Another success was the Darbishire Hall which was redesigned to provide a spacious and attractive area for the exhibition of textiles. As well as this, the North Gallery was remodelled with felicity, and two back galleries provided excellent accommodation for loan exhibitions—an action which helped to encourage the particularly energetic programmes

Fig 11 **North Gallery and Mezzanine** 1968

of loan exhibitions that were to follow. At the same time, an area adjacent to one of these back galleries was converted into a lecture hall, and was named after Sir Thomas Barlow who had given half a century's service to the Whitworth. The costs of the adaptation and furbishing (they amounted to about £15,000) were met by well-wishers and the Northern Arts (now the Granada) Foundation.

When the three envisaged stages of reconstruction had been completed, the formal opening of the Gallery was presided over by Lord Goodman in 1968. "Probably nowhere else in the British Isles" said the *Burlington Magazine* at the time, "could we discover such a successful and impressive attempt to transform a mausoleum into an agreeable modern art gallery". The *Financial Times* argued that, "It will doubtless fall to the Whitworth to provide the capital of the north with the important loan collections, and with such a splendid place available there is no reason why monumental shows planned for London... should not travel northwards". The *Daily*

efforts, had become a model of elegance for other galleries in the country. Some problems, however, still remained.

To begin with, the Whitworth had virtually no annual purchasing grant for works of art since, as we have seen, the original fund had been diverted to other purposes in the inter-war years and had never been replaced, though the Friends raised what they could. Professor Dodwell decided to alleviate this in 1969, by launching a public Appeal in Manchester and London, and his Appeal

Fig 12 **South Gallery** 1898

Fig 13 **South Gallery** 1968

Telegraph added that, "Since it was acquired by the University, the Whitworth has become one of the foremost of galleries", and in Paris the *Gazette des Beaux Arts* spoke of it being a new form of gallery which corresponded to certain forms of contemporary painting.

The rebuilding had taken some time, but now that it was over, the University of Manchester could relax a little and savour the knowledge that it had in its ownership a really fine gallery, one that was admired on all sides, and one that, as a result of the University's own innovative

achieved about £100,000 in terms of donations of money and works of art (which also were invited). The funds thus raised were later supplemented by a bequest from Margaret Pilkington and by monies from other non-University sources, but it must be said here that, despite the efforts of the past, the Gallery's purchasing fund remains sadly inadequate for an institute of our distinction.

Another problem was that such were the new and varied activities in the Gallery—not least the rapidly increasing number of loan exhibitions which the public found particularly attractive—that the curatorial staff set up in 1959/60 was rapidly seen to be insufficient—even as late as 1968 its total salaried strength consisted only of a Keeper, a Research Assistant, a Keeper of Textiles and an Assistant Keeper of Art. The University now had other developments to follow up, and in due course Professor Dodwell sought to correct the position by entering into personal negotiations with the Greater Manchester Council. Initially, it has to be said, they showed a marked reluctance, but gradually they came to respond to his requests and respond with such generosity that they enriched the whole life of the Gallery.

Most particularly, they agreed to his original request for staff, and this enabled him, over the years, virtually to double the strength of his salaried curatorial staff with the appointments of an Exhibitions Officer, a Gallery Services Officer, a Conservator, and a Wallpaper Curator, with, moreover, an exhibitions technician and a part-time exhibitions secretary added as well.

Over and above this, from 1974 onwards, the G.M.C. made annual grants both to help our exhibition programmes and to enhance our services to the public, and, in exchange, the Gallery circulated the considerable geographical area of the North West encompassed by the G.M.C. with exhibitions from its own collections. They further made *ad hoc* contributions to important projects and donated £35,000 towards the purchase of the seven sketch-books of John Robert Cozens that we were particularly anxious to acquire in 1975 (in this, we were also helped by the generosity of the Friends of the Whitworth, the National Art-Collections Fund, and the Pilgrim Trust). Again, the G.M.C. was one of the sponsors, in 1976, of the conversion of the upper floor of the Gallery which took the form of dividing the greater part of it into new and admirably furbished study rooms, one for the Department of Textiles and the other for the Department of Prints and Drawings; this development, let me add, was also assisted by contributions from the North West Museum and Art Gallery Service who have always been most generous to us. Finally, the Greater Manchester authority financed the furnishing and equipping of a new conservation room for the Gallery, and gave £100,000 towards an air conditioning plant for part of the building.

Given these circumstances, it came as a great shock to the staff of the Gallery to learn, in the Autumn of 1983, that this body, which had benefited us so much, was to be dissolved. However, in due course, negotiations took place between the University and the Minister of the Arts, the Earl of Gowrie, and we took comfort from his statement in the House of Lords that: "I am wholly confident that the Whitworth Art Gallery will not suffer reorganisation". In the event, the Government decided that the budgetary short-fall which resulted from the demise of the G.M.C. would be met by payments to the University through the University Grants Committee, and that, for three years, these grants would be ear-marked for the Gallery.

The Government, however, which had met our problem with some sympathy had a blow to deliver of its own, though this was not a direct one. It resulted from its decision to reduce the annual budgets of universities generally. Like most other universities, that of Manchester suffered, and from 1983, its annual grant from the University Grants Committee was cut back by 18%, which meant, in turn, that a similar cut was made in the annual grant given to the Whitworth by the University. Some retrenchment was necessarily forced on us as a result, and we lost four and a half non-curatorial staff, though the problems we had anticipated were much assuaged by a complete re-organisation of our security arrangements enabling us to economise on staff by using technical equipment. Our reduced financial position, I might add, had one positive result: it led us to undertake an even more vigorous programme of seeking sponsorship and raising money, and the launching of the highly successful Bistro—paying rent to the Gallery though not owned by it, and an admirable Gallery asset in itself—is an example of this form of self-help. Indeed, despite our earlier fears, we managed to weather the financial problems with every success and today the Whitworth Art Gallery is as robust as it has been at any time in its history.

As we have seen, it is a history that has witnessed many fluctuations of fortune, but despite them all, the Gallery has continued to go from strength to strength since being transferred to the University. Since then—or rather since the completion of the rebuilding in 1968—we have built up our collections by perceptive purchases, each head of a Department making the relevant annual choices subject to the agreement of the Director. As well as rotating displays from our own permanent collections, we have put on five or six important loan exhibitions each year, and have indeed built up a great reputation for ourselves as a centre for exhibitions. These have included many of national and international importance—from Switzerland, Holland, Belgium, Iran, the U.S.A., the U.S.S.R., Hungary and Czechoslovakia—some of them specially selected by our own staff within the country concerned, like the exhibition of European Master Drawings from the Hermitage (the first exhibition of pre-Revolutionary art that the Hermitage allowed to be sent to the West). At the same time, we have become reasonably well known abroad because of the exhibitions from our permanent collections that we have sent to different countries on the Continent, and because of the numerous loans of our works of art that we make to centres all over the world. We have also encouraged contemporary art, and every year have put on one, if not two, exhibitions in this field as well as supporting student art by organising the biennial *Whitworth* (formerly *Northern) Young Contemporaries* exhibitions, which offer prizes and prestige exhibition space for art students from the whole of Great Britain. With the help of the Friends of the Whitworth and the Whitworth Arts Society, we have arranged numerous lectures each year, and with the assistance of the Faculty of Music we have also put on regular concerts. We have succeeded, too, in maintaining close links with the History of Art Department of the University and not least with its prestigious post-graduate course which trains the art-curators of the future.

Where our own future as a Gallery is concerned, we look forward to our second century with optimism, and the fact that an Appeal is in progress for an extension to the Gallery under the patronage of the Prince of Wales indicates the buoyancy of our expectations as we look ahead. And as for myself, if I may end on a personal note, I might remark that, having come to the Gallery in 1966 when it was in the middle of a great programme of restructuring, I am gratified to think that, when I retire from the office of Honorary Director in the year of the Whitworth's centenary, it may well be again to the accompaniment of more Gallery building.   CR Dodwell

Embroidered Panel

Egypt: late 4th century

Dyed wools on linen ground 275 x 260mm
On permanent loan from the Manchester Museum (T.MM.252.1968)

Amongst the Coptic textiles transferred to the Whitworth on permanent loan from the Manchester Museum in the 1960s were two extremely rare embroidered panels depicting half-length females. They appear to be part of a group which represent the 'Seasons', this panel personifying Autumn and the other Winter. The 'Seasons' were a very popular subject in Roman art between the second and fifth centuries A.D. and are found, for example, in the mosaic pavements of Antioch. Each 'Season' is identified by an attribute; Winter carries a bare twig and Autumn fruit, here laden on a cloth and worn in her hair.

The dating of the panels is largely based on stylistic evidence. During the period of their probable manufacture Egypt was a Roman province, but when the Empire was divided in 394 the province was ruled from Constantinople, the Eastern capital of the Empire, and was thus exposed for several centuries to the influence of Byzantine culture. The panels certainly possess all the characteristics of late Antique art, and the deep-set eyes and modelling of the features is reminiscent of Byzantine portraits. The drop earrings which the woman wears are found in tapestry-woven portrait busts and other female figures of the late fourth and fifth centuries. Tapestry-woven 'Seasons' from the same period have also survived in other museum collections.

The source from which the panels came was associated with the excavations at Akhmîm on the right bank of the Nile in Upper Egypt, but they need not necessarily have been made there, since there was no tradition of embroidery in Egypt before the Islamic period. Tapestry weaving is far and away the most common technique among Egyptian patterned textiles. The technique actually used in the panels is interesting. It covers the ground completely in a manner similar to *opus anglicanum*, the renowned English embroidery of the thirteenth and fourteenth centuries. At first sight it appears to be chain-stitch embroidery, but examination under a stereozoom microscope reveals that the chain appearance is created by the close conjunction of two-ply S-twisted woollen threads which are couched down side by side.

Two or three pieces of Coptic embroidery (at the most) from this early period are recorded in other collections, but these appear to be of rather later date and are of inferior workmanship, making the two Manchester panels unique survivals. JH

Altar Frontal

Germany (Cologne region): late 15th century

Wool and silk tapestry, with metal threads, on linen warps;
paint on faces 890 x 2045mm
Purchased in 1891 (Sir J.C. Robinson's collection) (T.8247)

Sir John Charles Robinson evidently regarded this tapestry-woven altar frontal from the Cologne region in Germany as one of his finest acquisitions, for, in a letter of 3 December 1890 to Sir Joseph Lee regarding the purchase of his collection for the Whitworth, he declared himself "under the strongest temptation to keep this last purchase in the series". It is certainly a very finely woven piece and, for its date, in wonderful condition.

The subject represented is the Tree of Jesse, which translates into pictorial form the prophecy of Isaiah: "And there shall come forth a rod out of the stem of Jesse, and a Branch shall grow out of his roots" (Isaiah, 11, v.1). The Tree is depicted growing from the chest of the centrally seated figure of Jesse, its spiralling branches enclosing the figures of the twelve Kings of Israel, the actual and spiritual ancestors of Christ. They are identified by the scrolls which they hold bearing their names, as Abia and Reheboam, Asa and Solomon, and Jehosaphat and David, to the left of Jesse and, to the right, Joram and Manarsah, Ahazia and Hezekiah, and Jotham and Ahaz. The figures appear to grow like flowers from formalised sepals on a slender stalk, a convention which is paralleled in South German manuscripts of the same date. In keeping with medieval practice, there is no attempt at clothing these biblical figures in historically plausible attire. Their richly patterned dress, hair-style and headgear are contemporary, and both confirm the German origins of the tapestry and suggest a production date c.1470.

At the top, above the figure of Jesse, is the crowned Virgin and Child and, in each corner, are the emblems of the four Evangelists, the angel of St. Matthew, the lion of St. Mark, the calf of St. Luke, and the eagle of St. John. The border above the tapestry, however, which acts as a superfrontal, is a later, possibly sixteenth-century, addition, and depicts the Nativity with the figures of Saints Catherine and Barbara at either end. The inscription reads: PUER NATUS EST NOBIS ET FILIUS DATUS EST NOBIS (Unto us a Boy is Born, Unto us a Son is Given).

This prophecy of Isaiah was taken, from the third century onwards, to be a reference to Christ's incarnation. The Tree of Jesse was a popular subject in art in the late Middle Ages and appears frequently in stained glass and embroidery, as well as in painting and sculpture.   JH

Four Women Dancing c1497

Engraving attributed to Zoan Andrea
(working 1475-1519) Italian

Engraving; plate mark 224 x 344 mm

Presented by G.T. Clough in 1921 (3131)

The four figures in this engraving are taken from a painting by Andrea Mantegna (1431-1506), known as *Parnassus*. The painting was commissioned by Isabella d'Este Gonzaga as part of a suite to decorate her private study in the palace at Mantua. The painting's subject is the love affair between Venus and Mars, and the jealousy of Vulcan, who, enraged by Venus' infidelity, trapped the two lovers in bed with a bronze net, and displayed them for the amusement of the other gods. The illicit love affair was encouraged by Mercury and Apollo. They are shown in the painting on the mountain of Parnassus with a group of nine female figures, thought to be the Muses, dancing beneath the arched rock on which the two lovers, Venus and Mars, are standing. The Muses were Greek deities of poetry, literature, music and astronomy; Zoan Andrea has used four of the nine dancing figures in his print.

This print reveals much about the ways in which engraving was used in Italy only a few decades after the technique was first introduced into the peninsula. Methods of engraving and printing from copper plates became known in Italy some decades after their invention in northern Europe. It is not known exactly when or how this knowledge spread but Zoan Andrea's print was certainly produced within the first fifty years of Italian experimentation with the technique. Like the majority of engravings produced in Mantua at this time, its style as well as its subject matter is based heavily on the work of Andrea Mantegna. Mantegna was an immensely influential and celebrated artist who, from the age of about thirty, had spent his life as court painter to the Gonzaga Marquesses of Mantua. Mantegna's drawings were greatly in demand by other artists as sources of poses for figures, etc, and it was probably their popularity that first suggested the production of this type of engraving, which reproduced quite closely the open parallel lines of shading characteristic of Mantegna's style of pen drawing. Indeed, since the poses of the four dancing women in Andrea's print vary slightly from Mantegna's finished painting, it is thought that the engraver was copying from a preparatory drawing by Mantegna rather than from the finished painting.

Mantegna must have realised the financial gains to be made from using engraving to multiply his own drawings in this way. Not only did he produce engravings in the style of his own pen drawings, but he also provided numerous other printmakers with drawings to use as models, and a whole school of engravers seems to have grown up, their style marked by their .attempts to reproduce Mantegna's drawings as closely as possible. However, it is also possible that Mantegna wanted to keep a very close eye on works produced after his designs and surviving letters suggest that Zoan Andrea and another engraver, called Simone di Ardizone, may have been the targets of persecution by Mantegna. This may have stemmed from personal antagonism, but it may equally have been prompted by Mantegna's anger at the two engravers producing unauthorized copies of Mantegna's work.

Engravings such as ours were hugely popular in Italy when they were first produced, and they seem to have been printed in large numbers. Unfortunately, the extent of their popularity, and perhaps also their practical function as a source of figure poses and designs for practising artists, meant that they were not necessarily treated with great care. As a result, early Italian prints only survive today in small numbers. The Whitworth is very fortunate in owning a number of them. SH

20

Melencolia I 1514
Designed and engraved by
Albrecht Dürer (1471-1528) German
Engraving; second state of two; plate mark 140 x 290 mm

Presented by G.T. Clough in 1921 (3018)

Dürer's engraving shows a brooding, winged female figure, surrounded by an extraordinary collection of figures and objects; one scholar, Erwin Panofsky, in fact described this print as "Dürer's most perplexing engraving". However, Panofsky's researches have given us some idea of the meanings which Dürer's image might have held when it was first issued. It seems to rely on two major literary and artistic traditions: the four humours, and the seven liberal arts, and from them Dürer has isolated the humour of melancholy, and the discipline of geometry.

Writings by Renaissance scholars had, by the time that Dürer began his career, gradually changed the associations hitherto attached to the humour of melancholy. Associated with black bile and the god Saturn, it had in earlier centuries been the most dreaded of the four humours, responsible, it was thought, for depressive states of mind leading to insanity. Recent Florentine philosophers however, had asserted that all truly outstanding people were melancholics. The latter, they said, were indeed both easily excited and easily depressed, but they also had periods of outstanding creativity unknown in other types of people. Humanist writers had also re-assessed the image of the god Saturn, whom they saw as representing the mind, and therefore superior even to Jupiter, who symbolised the soul. It is Saturn who provides the link between melancholy and geometry. As god of the earth, Saturn was associated with work in stone and wood, and with agricultural activities such as the partitioning of land, which involved geometry.

These new views help us to understand some of the meanings of Dürer's image. Since, for Dürer, the principles of geometry were fundamental to his own work as an artist, the print's subject relates to both geometry and art. The reason why a figure representing these two disciplines should be shown as a melancholic again stems from the writings of Renaissance philosophers, who characterised artists as having minds more capable of imagination than able to understand abstract concepts. They might master mathematics, but they could not grasp metaphysical ideas; they could only deal with concepts which have actual physical existence, spatial or quantitative. This inability leads them to frustration and depression.

It is for this reason that Dürer's winged figure is shown as having exceptional abilities in the fields of art and geometry, but as being unable to use them or to find any comfort in them. Panofsky has described the image as typifying

the artist of the Renaissance who respects practical skill, but longs all the more fervently for mathematical theory— who feels 'inspired' by celestial influences and eternal ideas, but suffers all the more deeply from... human frailty and intellectual finiteness.

This interpretation is supported by more detailed meanings attributable to the objects surrounding Melencolia. The tools and instruments represent geometry, as do the stone geometrical shapes to her right. The animals in the scene allude to the melancholic humour— dogs were thought to be subject to depression and madness, and bats, preferring darkness, represented the melancholic element. Melancholics were also thought to have dark complexions and Dürer has therefore cast the woman's face in deep shadow. This device heightens the effect of the bright whites of her staring eyes and, since hers are the only eyes visibly open (the child is looking down and the dog sleeps), her isolation is dramatically emphasised. On her head Melencolia wears a wreath of 'watery' plants (water parsley and water cress) to protect against the harmful effects of Saturn's (ie the earth's) dryness. Similarly, the magic square of numbers behind her, all the columns of which add up to thirty-four, was a talisman used to attract the healing influences of Jupiter. From Melencolia's belt hang a bunch of keys and a purse, symbols of the power and wealth which should be the rewards of an artist who studies and works hard, but which here hang useless at her side.   SH

22

Funeral Cope

Spain: mid-16th century

Black velvet with silk appliqué 1372 x 2794 mm
Purchased in 1891 (Sir J.C. Robinson's Collection) (T.8045)

This Spanish funeral cope of the mid-sixteenth century is one of the finest and most unusual of the ecclesiastical vestments originally in the collection of Sir John Charles Robinson (1824-1913), which formed the basis of the Whitworth's present textile collection. Robinson's collection was especially rich in ecclesiastical embroideries, purchased chiefly in Spain and Italy, where the suppression of religious establishments during the 1870s brought unusual quantities of church property on to the art market. Writing of his collection on 19 July 1888, Robinson noted that the "sources of acquisition of the principal specimens have been the sacristies and treasuries of Cathedrals and suppressed Monasteries", but added that supplies from these sources had by then been exhausted, so that fine specimens were as difficult to come by as before.

The cope's black velvet ground is covered with a diaper pattern of acanthus stems and leaves, which have been applied separately and embroidered over in yellow silk. Appliqué was a favourite technique of the sixteenth and seventeenth centuries. In line with traditional practice it is the hood and orphreys of the cope which bear the most important and symbolic embroidery. These have skulls and crossed bones of silk appliqué which, together with the colour, indicate the function of the vestment.

Liturgical colours were first observed from about the twelfth century, but for the most important festivals many churches continued to use those vestments which were in the best condition or made of the richest fabrics. Black, however, was reserved for Good Friday and for general mourning, and the rather macabre iconography of this particular vestment would forbid its use at other church festivals.

The cope underwent extensive conservation at the Area Museums Service in the 1970s. When the lining was removed evidence was discovered of several earlier linings as well as considerable accretions of candle wax, suggesting continual use of the vestment over a long period. It was also discovered, on closer examination, that the embroidered ground motifs had originally been worked on a yellow patterned silk.

In the Western church the cope is a ceremonial garment and has never been a proper liturgical vestment. It can be worn by all ranks of clergy, and not just the priest officiating at Mass, and thus it is often worn on processions and at non-Eucharist ceremonies such as christenings, marriages and funerals. As it evolved into a ceremonial robe from a protective outdoor garment, the hood ceased to be functional and was eventually reduced to a vestigial flap at the back.   JH

Panel from a coat

Persia: c1600

Lampas weave silk on satin ground 1485 x 355 mm
Provenance unknown (T.8276)

This long panel of silk lampas appears to represent the side front from a long Persian coat, most probably a man's. Other pieces of the same design are in the Victoria and Albert Museum, London, the Musée Historique des Tissus, Lyon, and the Musée des Arts Décoratifs in Paris. Its design is characteristic of a group of silks and velvets woven in Persia under the Safavid dynasty (1499-1722) which take as their subject groups of human figures, unusual in textile design at this period.

The pattern repeat is made up of two groups of figures enclosed by flowering stems, which signify that they are in a garden. It reminds one of the enchanted world of the *Arabian Nights*. In the top half of the repeat a servant offers a bottle of rose water to a young man seated on a throne whilst, below, another young man, seated cross-legged on the ground, is offered a dish of pomegranates by a kneeling servant. The whole is shown against a black ground, which is a distinguishing feature of many of these textiles. The garden is a potent symbol in Persian poetry, mysticism and theological thought, and was kept cool and shaded for contemplation. Depictions of the garden in contemporary painting are also often shown against a dark or night sky, and it may be this aspect of the garden which is suggested by the dark ground in the textiles.

Persian textiles continued to make extensive use of figurative subjects when neighbouring Turkey and western Europe had adopted non-figural floral and geometric patterns. This figurative style undoubtedly reflects the influence of contemporary miniature painting with its illustrations of epic and legendary themes, although it is difficult to link the textile designs to specific paintings. Manuscript painting in Persia had already attained a high level of sophistication by the fifteenth century, and the Safavid rulers were highly cultivated art lovers who fostered a close interaction between all the arts. It is not unlikely that painters would also be responsible for designs for textiles.

The textiles are difficult to date other than by stylistic comparison with contemporary painting, but the lively narrative scenes of battle and hunting are traditionally ascribed to the mid-sixteenth century, and the more peaceful genre scenes depicting figures in landscape settings to the reign of Shah Abbas (1587-1629). Under this ruler silk weaving became Persia's major industry. Seventeenth-century European travellers mention Yezd, Kashan and Isfahan as being centres of silk-weaving, and the silk textiles with figure subjects were particularly associated with Isfahan. Shah Abbas moved the capital from Qazim, in the north, to Isfahan in 1598 to avoid the constant threat from the Ottoman Turks, and a court manufactory was established there at the beginning of the seventeenth century.

Persian silks of this period are amongst the finest, artistically and technically, of all decorative textiles. As well as supplying local needs, these luxury textiles were also exported, and elements of Safavid design were later incorporated into the western European design tradition, particularly the use of certain naturalistic floral motifs such as carnations. JH

Casket 1654-6

Embroidered by Hannah Smith British

Wood casket covered with satin and canvas embroidered in floss silks,
metal threads, purl, spangles and seed pearls 305 x 177 x 255mm
Purchased in 1891 (Sir J.C. Robinson's Collection) (T.8237)

Hannah Smith's casket is the earliest dated example of the richly embroidered boxes or cabinets, the making of which became almost a craze in the half a century between 1650 and 1700. It is so called after the signatory of a letter which was found in one of its drawers and which records the time and place of its making:

*the yere of our Lord being 1657; if ever I have any
thoughts about the time when I went to Oxford...
my being there near 2 yers; for I went in 1654 and
I stayed there 1655 and I cam away in 1656; and I was
almost 12 yers of age when I went; and I made an end
of my cabinete at Oxford ... and my cabinet was mad
up in the yere of 1656 at London; I have ritten this
to fortiffy my self and those that shall inquir about
it; Hannah Smith*

The front doors of the casket open to reveal one full-width drawer, three narrower drawers and a wide, locked panel. Two of the three narrow drawers are shorter in length than the third and, when removed and the divider eased out, a 'secret' drawer is revealed at the rear. Under the lid of the casket is a recess for writing materials.

Unlike later caskets, where 'stumpwork' (raised embroidery) predominates, the top, sides and doors of Hannah Smith's casket are embroidered in a variety of different techniques. The panels on the two front doors represent scenes from the Old Testament: on the left, the story of Deborah and Barak and, on the right, Jael and Sisera (Judges IV). They are worked in fine tent and rococo stitches on a canvas ground, and are similar to the small needlework pictures of biblical subjects with which they are contemporary. The two side panels of the casket represent Summer and Winter, personified by a female figure harvesting corn and an old man and his cat warming themselves by a fire. Here, laid satin and long and short stitches create less geometric and more naturalistic effects than the tent-stitched canvas, and there is a more subtle blending of colours.

The panel on the lid, which depicts Joseph raised from the pit and sold by his brothers to the Midianite merchants (Genesis XXXVII), is the most complex panel technically. The figure of Joseph is in raised work, one of the earliest dated examples of the technique in England. The composition is taken from one of the engraved plates in the *Thesaurus Sacrarum Historiarum Veteris Testamenti* of Gerard de Jode, a volume of Bible illustrations published in Antwerp in 1589 which seems to have been widely used by seventeenth-century embroideresses; many needle-worked versions of the engravings are known. Similarly, the cat on the side panel of the casket was taken from one of the books of natural history which, from the sixteenth century, were supplementing the bestiaries and herbals of the Middle Ages. It appears in both the first volume of Conrad Gesner's *Icones Animalium* (1551) and in Edward Topsell's *Historie of Four-Footed Beasts* (1607).

Although embroideresses did occasionally make tracings directly from such books of engravings, by the middle of the seventeenth century it was possible to buy from printsellers printed sheets of pattern designs which asssimilated published material from a variety of sources. These direct, line-for-line borrowings from a wide variety of publications result in the discrepancy of scale which one finds in the majority of domestic embroideries of this date.

According to Hannah Smith's letter, when the needlework was complete, the embroidery was sent to a cabinet maker who would fix it on to a casket of a previously agreed design. These seem to have been made up to a stock pattern since, in many of the surviving cabinets, even the 'secret' drawers are in the same place.

A casket was the crowning achievement in a series of projects, beginning with simple lettering samplers, that made up a girl's education as a needlewoman in the seventeenth century. Hannah Smith's letter reinforces the evidence for these caskets having been the work of girls rather than adult needlewomen, and provides valuable information on the making of them.   JH

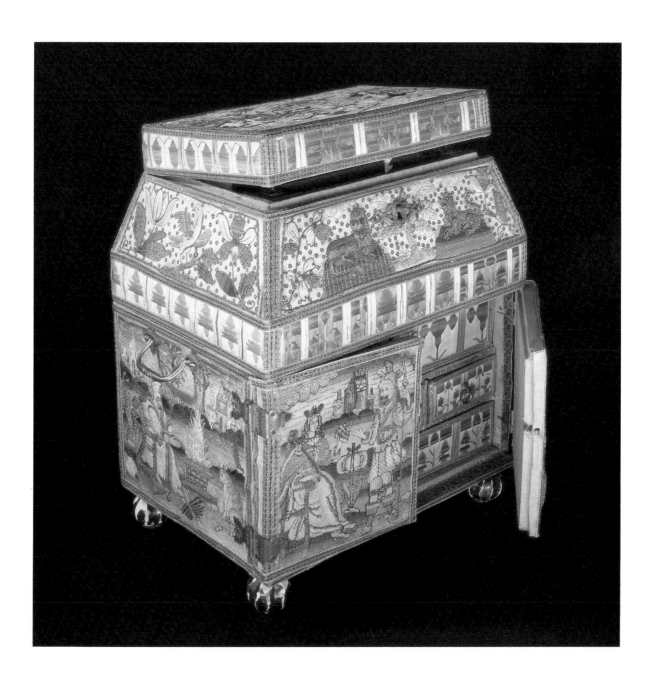

The Three Crosses c1660-1

Designed and engraved by
Rembrandt Harmensz van Rijn (1606-1669) Dutch

Drypoint and engraving; fourth state of five; plate mark 383 x 450 mm

Presented by G.T. Clough in 1929 (5040)

Rembrandt's image shows a central figure of Christ on the cross; his body, and that of the robber crucified to his right are just visible in the gloomy light, whilst the third crucified figure to Christ's left is almost obliterated by darkness. At the foot of the cross are two Roman soldiers mounted on horseback, the most prominent, in a high-crowned hat, being a centurion.

The print is a remarkable one in many ways, not least because of its size and technique; the image measures 380×450mm (15x17¾ inches) and is executed almost entirely in drypoint. This is a printmaking method akin to engraving, but instead of using a metal tool, to cut a crisp V-shaped incision into the metal printing plate, drypoint work is carried out by scratching with a sharp, needle-like tool into the surface of the copper. As the needle scores the plate it will throw up tiny curls of copper known as 'burr'. When the plate is inked and printed, this burr will hold quantities of ink, and will print the rich, dark, smudgy lines which are essential to this print's impact. The main disadvantage of the drypoint technique is that the burr is very fragile and will wear down after being passed through a printing press, if only twenty times, producing thinner, paler lines which have lost all their dramatic impact. Because of this, most printmakers were unwilling to use drypoint except to create local accents of shadow in an image mainly produced by etching or engraving; it was most unusual for a printmaker to create an entire image out of drypoint, and rare indeed to use it to create an image of this size.

The large copper plate from which *The Three Crosses* was printed has a surprising history. Rembrandt first started work on it in 1653, producing and printing an image of a particular stage in the story of Christ's crucifixion. Some years later, however, he burnished out much of his earlier image, and re-worked the plate in drypoint to present a quite different moment in the Crucifixion story. Our own impression of the print was taken after Rembrandt had carried out this re-working; the significance of the image, however, can best be understood by considering the differences between the scene shown in the earlier version and in ours.

For the earlier image, Rembrandt followed the description of the Crucifixion given in St Luke's Gospel, depicting the moment of Christ's death and the conversion of the Roman centurion who is shown kneeling at the foot of the Cross, his arms outstretched in wonder:

And when Jesus had cried with a loud voice, he said, Father, into thy hands I commend my spirit: and having said thus he gave up the ghost.
Now when the centurion saw what was done, he glorified God, saying, Certainly this was a righteous man.

When Rembrandt came back to the plate, one of the main alterations he made to it was to change the figure of the centurion; he is now shown mounted on horseback, advancing gravely towards the Cross. Rembrandt also changed his biblical source, this time taking the account from St Matthew's or St Mark's Gospel. The shafts of light which had illuminated the earlier state of the print have disappeared, and we now see the moment described by Matthew as follows:

Now from the sixth hour there was darkness over all the land unto the ninth hour. And about the ninth hour Jesus cried with a loud voice... My God, my God, why has thou forsaken me?

It is at this moment that we are made most aware of Christ's human frailty rather than his divine nature. Whereas in the earlier image Rembrandt showed the moment of Christ's death, and the hopeful sign for the future of Christianity provided by the conversion of the centurion, he has here represented an earlier stage, when Christ was alive but undergoing a deep spiritual crisis. It is the pain of this moment that Rembrandt has tried to convey through the deep drypoint scorings which produce the harrowing darkness of the image.   SH

Stag Hunting Scene
England: c1680-1700

Fragment of wallpaper, block printed outline
with stencilled colours 395 x 440 mm
Presented by the Wall Paper Manufacturers Limited in 1967 (W.26a.1967)

Dating from c.1680, this fragment is one of the oldest of the wallpapers in the Whitworth's collection. It came to the Gallery in 1967 as part of the Wall Paper Manufacturers' presentation having been originally acquired, along with two other very similar fragments (W.26 b.& c.1967), by Mr Eric Entwisle, a Director of the company, in 1952. According to Mr Entwisle, all three fragments relate to a building known as Aldford House which was situated in Park Lane, London. However, as with so many examples of historic wallcoverings no documentation exists and the exact provenance of this sheet has proved impossible to determine. We do know that Aldford House (demolished in 1931) was not built until 1894-7, and that prior to that time the site was occupied by residences that were erected during and after 1739. This post-dates the production of this wallpaper by some fifty years and it is therefore extremely unlikely that it was used as a decoration in either the early or later Aldford House. The current view is that it simply belonged to one of the tenants.

The fragment depicts a lively stag-hunting scene, with horsemen and dogs pursuing their prey through a landscape crowded with trees, houses, birds and with a village pond. To modern eyes the pictorial design would seem to be a rather unusual choice for a wallpaper. A brief review of the history and origins of paperhangings, however, will help to explain the somewhat curious appearance of this example.

By the end of the fifteenth century, the manufacture of paper was sufficiently advanced for it to be produced in large quantities and at comparatively low prices all over Europe. The possibility of using it for purposes other than printing books and illustrations soon suggested itself and c.1500 examples of wallpaper began to appear. The earliest surviving piece was produced in England c.1509 and decorated rooms in the Master's Lodge at Christ's College, Cambridge. It was printed from engraved wooden blocks which were first inked and then covered with hand-made paper which was pressed down onto the block. Wallpaper manufacture changed little over the next hundred or so years and the *Aldford House* fragments were produced in exactly the same way, except that they contain areas of colour that were applied through specially cut stencils.

Initially, the chief attraction of wallpapers was their cheapness, especially in comparison to other wallcoverings such as tapestries, painted cloths and leather hangings. Even so, the custom of using long lengths of printed paper to decorate the walls of major apartments did not become widespread until the eighteenth century. Earlier examples more often than not had crudely-drawn designs that were printed on small rectangular sheets of paper, and were used only in lesser rooms and later as lining papers for boxes and cupboards. The *Aldford House* fragments may well have been intended to serve both functions. Almost identical versions of the stag-hunting scene have been found adorning the walls of a first-floor room in a house in Epsom, and also lining the interior of a deed-box at Clandon Park. Other variants of the design are now in the Victoria and Albert Museum and at Colonial Williamsburg, Virginia.

The use of a pictorial design was not, in fact, particularly unusual in wallpapers of the sixteenth and seventeenth centuries. Comparatively few examples from this period employed ornamental motifs, and many were more akin to woodcut illustrations than to conventional repeating wallpaper designs. Moreover, the *Aldford House* fragments have recently been compared to contemporary tapestry and needlework pictures and it is quite possible that the inspiration for the stag-hunting scene came from this source.   JB

The Musicians c1690-1710

Designed by Jean-Baptiste Monnoyer (1636-1699) French
Woven at Beauvais, France

Wool and silk woven tapestry 2010 x 2690mm
Purchased in 1986 with the aid of grants from the Victoria and Albert Museum Purchase Grant Fund,
the National Art-Collections Fund and the Friends of the Whitworth (T.28.1986)

The Musicians is one of a series of tapestries woven at Beauvais in France towards the end of the seventeenth century and commonly known as the *Grotesques de Berain*. The tapestry works at Beauvais came into particular prominence during the management of Philippe Behagle, who became its second director in 1684. He employed Jean Berain (1637-1711) and other leading artists to design several new sets of figurative tapestries. The *Grotesques* was the most popular and financially successful of the twenty or so series produced under Behagle. They were still being ordered long after his death in 1705, and over 150 pieces have been recorded.

The series was usually made in sets of six pieces, whose subjects represent apparently unrelated groups of strolling players, animal tamers and musicians in contemporary theatrical costume. They resemble, although they cannot be firmly identified with, actors in the famous *Commedia dell'Arte*. The term *Grotesques* was used in its sixteenth-century sense to refer to the random mythological figures and type of decoration found on the original borders to the tapestries, which were modelled on antique Roman wall-paintings copied in the sixteenth century by Raphael. The heavy strapwork design of the border on the Whitworth's *Musicians* was a variant.

The dull yellow ground on which the tapestries were worked, called *tabac d'Espagne* in French and sometimes Havana yellow in English, was especially popular in the 1680s. The designs must have been completed by 1689 as, in that year, several panels from the series were used as security for a loan by Behagle. It is more difficult to determine the precise date at which the Whitworth's tapestry was woven, but since it bears Behagle's signature in the bottom right-hand corner it may safely be assumed that it was woven under his direction, or under that of his widow and son who bore the same name (1705-11). Stylistically, the *Grotesques* reflect a move away from the sombre gravity of tapestry design under Louis XIV towards the more light-hearted decorative style associated with the period of *Régence* (1714-26).

Although it is possible that Jean Berain inspired the choice of subject since there are compositional similarities with ornamental prints by the artist, the cartoons for the *Grotesques* were actually the work of the flower painter Jean-Baptiste Monnoyer. Like the other subjects in the series, *The Musicians* is richly decorated with the flowers that were Monnoyer's speciality.

Under the patronage of Louis XIV and his finance minister Colbert, French tapestry acquired, in the latter part of the seventeenth century, a pre-eminent place among the luxury industries of Europe. Colbert set up the Gobelins in 1662 as a royal manufactory, and the Beauvais works two years later, primarily to cater for private customers rather than for the Crown. It was, therefore, intended to be a commercial enterprise and Behagle had to produce what his customers were willing to pay for. One requirement was that tapestries should fit the walls where they were intended to hang. The *Grotesques* were admirably designed to accommodate such customers, and could be curtailed in either height or width or both. The *Musicians*, for example, forms the centre section of a wide tapestry called *The Camel* and was one of the most popular sections to be treated in this way.

In 1695 a set of *Grotesques* was commissioned for the Swedish Chancellor, Count Carl Piper, which were shorter in height than usual and which had borders after a design by Jean Berain. A letter concerning the commission from Daniel Cronström in Paris to Nicodemus Tessin in Sweden, describes "une bordeure... du dessein de Berain, à bastons rompus rouges sur un fond bleu". The description accords perfectly with the strapwork design on the Whitworth's tapestry which, as it happens, is also curtailed in height. It is tempting to conjecture that the Whitworth's *Musicians* formerly belonged to the set commissioned for Piper, but it should be said that the Berain border does also appear on other surviving examples of the design.   JH

Embossed Leather Hanging

France: early 18th century

Embossed with a heated metal plate, gilded and hand-painted 710 x 510 mm

Presented by the Wall Paper Manufacturers Limited in 1967 (W.103.1967)

The history of wallcoverings has included many media besides that of paper. Painted stencils, flocked canvas and woven hangings have all been used at one time or another to decorate the walls of our historic homes. Perhaps the most unlikely, and certainly the least documented of these alternatives, however, is embossed and gilded leather which was used extensively as a wallhanging throughout the seventeenth and eighteenth centuries. This panel is one of several in the Gallery's collection. Not only is it a fine and well-preserved example of the leather gilder's art but it also provides a useful opportunity to review the origins and development of this subject.

The art of leather gilding is an ancient one. It was first practised by the Islamic peoples of North Africa who introduced it into Europe in the eleventh century following the Moorish invasion of Spain. For many years Spain remained the major supplier of leather hangings but at the outset of the seventeenth century, production shifted to Holland and the Low Countries, and later to France, Italy and England. While each country developed its own style of decoration and range of designs, certain patterns appear to have been especially popular and were exchanged between different centres of manufacture. This panel, for example, was produced in France, but almost identical versions with the distinctive tasselled canopy, scrolling foliage and urn of flowers, have been found in Spain, Holland, Flanders and England.

The leather used for embossed and gilded hangings was usually calf-skin, tanned and cut into rectangular panels of approximately 600 x 750mm. Each panel was sized and the smoother side covered with silver or tin foil, which was then treated with yellow varnish to give the impression of bright and costly gold. Finally, parts of the design were hand-coloured with oil paint and glazes.

The embossing was done in one of two ways; either by using heated iron or copper plates, or wooden moulds. With the first process, the leather was pressed down onto the plate and into the engraved design. With the second, it was dampened and then passed through a heavy roller press between a mould and countermould carved with complementary sections of the pattern. Wooden moulds were cheap to use and to make, and they produced hangings with an impressively high relief. Their disadvantage, though, was that they were unable to achieve the same delicacy of drawing and detail that can be found in this example which has obviously been embossed with an engraved metal plate.

Although a few surviving panels date from the thirteenth century, leather hangings did not become truly popular until the early seventeenth. From that time on they were a standard accessory in many of Europe's wealthiest and most fashionable homes, and the remarks of an Italian, Leonardo Fioraventi, in 1586, bear witness to the fortunes that could be made from practising this art. "Leather gilding", he writes, "is an art of great profit and knowledge by means of which one makes friends with great personages; for the greater part of those who use it are illustrious and great because the art is very beautiful to behold. It is not without good cause that the art is called gilding, because the design is drawn in gold and silver, and it makes rich those who practise it in a skilful manner."

In spite of these aristocratic associations, embossed and gilded leather did not remain in favour much past the third or fourth decade of the eighteenth century. The richness and solidity of its appearance which, along with its durability, had originally been the qualities that had so appealed to an upper- and middle-class clientele, later made them unacceptable in interiors now decorated in a light and delicate Rococo style. Many hangings were therefore discarded around this time, or banished to the less visible areas of the house such as the passageways or stairs, but some extremely fine examples can still be seen today at Dyrham Park, Chatsworth, Kingston Lacy and other stately homes.   JB

Bridal Cushion Cover

Greece (Epirus): 18th century

Linen embroidered in coloured silks and gilt metal thread 381 x 711 mm
Bequeathed by Sir Joseph Lee in 1930 (T.8130)

Traditionally in Greece and the Greek Islands, a girl's dowry would include a collection of embroidery worked largely by herself, which would figure in the marriage contract. It consisted in the main of household articles, the most important of which were furnishings for the marriage bed. As well as bed curtains the bed would be piled high with ornamental cushions or pillows with richly embroidered covers. These bridal cushion covers were the *chef d'oeuvre* of a girl's dower chest.

Following the traditional arrangement, this example from Epirus in the north-western part of mainland Greece depicts the bride and bridegroom, side by side and in their wedding clothes. Between them is a large coffee pot. Sometimes the bridal couple appears as part of a procession, accompanied by their parents and attendants. The rest of the ground is filled with stylised cypress trees, flowers and birds.

The main sources of influence on the patterns and motives of Greek and Greek island embroidery were Byzantine, Persian, Turkish and Western European (particularly Italian) designs, which were assimilated into easily identifiable local styles. Turkish influence was particularly strong in Epirus, which came under Turkish rule in the fifteenth century and remained so until its return to the kingdom of Greece in 1912. Most of the floral motifs in embroidery from Epirus reflect Turkish influence, especially the carnation and hyacinth, which are used in the narrow scrolling stem border on this cushion cover and which predominate in the main ground.

Flowers in Turkish textiles, however, owe a great deal in their turn to the textile designs of Safavid Persia (1499-1722). The men's costume on the bridal cushion covers is similar to that described as Turkish in sixteenth-century costume books, and Turkish dress was possibly the costume of the Epirote bourgeoisie.

Although the costume on the cushion cover may represent Epirote costume of the sixteenth century, it does not follow that the embroidery is to be dated as early as this. A conservative attitude to design is a chief characteristic of any peasant art, and traditional patterns were handed down in Greece from generation to generation. Thus, the motif of the bridal couple could easily have continued in use long after fashions in actual dress had changed. Whilst such traditionalism in pattern-making might be accounted for by the isolated geographical situation of the islands and the unchanging lifestyle of the island women, this was not true of Epirus. From the seventeenth to the nineteenth century Jannina, the capital of Epirus, was one of the leading towns of Greece, at times exceeding even Athens in size and importance. It reached the height of its prosperity under Ali Pasha in the late eighteenth and early nineteenth centuries, when it became a focal point for trade and communication betweeen East and West, and a centre for the luxury crafts. Because of this, and the fact that the practice of working embroideries for the dower chest died out soon afterwards, the bridal cushion covers of Epirus are traditionally dated to the eighteenth century.   JH

Petticoat
India: 1750-75

Painted and dyed cotton 1016 x 4267mm
Provenance unknown (T.8223)

From 1600 to 1800 India was the greatest exporter of textiles the world had then known, and fabrics like the one from which this petticoat is made were produced not for local use but for export to Europe, to be sold in Holland, England and France. It is not difficult to appreciate the attractions for the Europeans of the Indian painted and printed cottons, or 'chintz' as they were known (from the Hindu word 'chint' meaning 'coloured' or 'variegated'); by comparison with the velvets and silk brocades then in fashion, cotton dresses were light and soft to the touch; and before 1700 European block-printing techniques produced crude results and fugitive colours, whilst the patterns of Indian chintz were bright and skilfully drawn and the dyes fast, thereby allowing frequent washing.

The Indian craftsman had long been pre-eminent in the use of fixing agents, called mordants. In the West these were applied by means of wood blocks, whereas in India they were painted on to the cloth free-hand, although the increasing use of the word 'printed' during the eighteenth century does suggest the introduction of wood blocks into Indian manufacture also. Mordant dyeing was a complex and lengthy process which could take several weeks to complete. It involved the painstaking process of painting in all the flowers, birds and stems with a variety of different mordants—iron, alum, chrome, zinc, and tin—which, in reaction with a red dye obtained from chay (in Europe, from madder), gave the fabric its rich range of colours from black through crimson to pink. Those areas, on the other hand, which were required to be blue or green were left blank, and the rest of the cloth waxed to resist the indigo dye-bath. This elaborate process was necessary because indigo was not fast unless applied in the form of a dye-bath rather than by direct printing or painting. The wax was removed by scraping and washing. Yellow areas, possibly using saffron, were painted in by hand, whilst yellow painted over blue produced the greens. The glazed finish of much Indian chintz which is also a feature of this petticoat was achieved by rubbing the surface of the cloth with a shell until a high polish was produced.

Indian hand-painted cottons were first imported into England in quantity after 1600, the year that the English East India Company was founded. A century later they had become so popular that a law was passed in 1701 to protect the English silk and wool manufacturers; this forbade the importation, use and wearing of Indian chintz. The act was not repealed until 1764, but it was openly defied, and the majority of surviving pieces, like the Whitworth's petticoat, date, ironically enough, from the period of prohibition. Chintz first became popular for women's dress in the late seventeenth century, and remained a much coveted stuff for dress throughout the eighteenth century.

Around 1700 English printers began to try to produce simple copies of Indian work and, although their early efforts were rather crude, standards of English calico printing improved so rapidly in the eighteenth century that, by 1800, the earlier situation had been reversed and England had become the foremost exporter of printed cotton. However, throughout the seventeenth and eighteenth centuries, Indian patterns formed the basis of dress and furnishing fabric designs in Europe, whilst the techniques used to print them became the basis of the European dye systems.   JH

After the Marriage 1745

Plate II from Marriage à-la-Mode
Designed and published by William Hogarth (1697-1764) British
Engraved by Bernard Baron

Etching and engraving; third state of five; plate mark 405 x 560 mm
Provenance unknown

This plate is the second in a series of six prints which tells the story of the marriage of a young couple, from its arrangement by their parents, to the deaths of both partners, each from unnatural causes. The pair are here shown as newly-weds, but Hogarth indicates in a variety of ways that their marriage is already in difficulties. This, however, comes as little surprise after the signs given in the first plate that the marriage was arranged wholly for the benefit of the couple's parents; the girl's merchant father wanting the social status that her marriage to the son of an Earl would bring, and the Earl desperate for the hard cash that would come as part of the marriage settlement. The young couple themselves were shown to have not the slightest interest in each other.

Perhaps the clues which first show the viewer that all is not well are the poses and gestures of each of the four figures. Those of the young husband and wife eloquently express his depression and her boredom, whilst the slovenliness of the servant in the adjoining room, and the despairing gesture of the steward, who carries with him a pile of unpaid bills and only one receipt, suggest that the couple neglect their household affairs as well as their marriage. Supporting this impression are objects strewn around the room which suggest the quite separate activities in which husband and wife have been engaged. The candles in the chandelier in the far room seem to have been burning all night, indicating that the time 1.20 on the clock is an early morning hour; the cards on the floor and the book *Hoyle on Whist* at her feet show that the young wife has been holding a card party at her home, whilst her husband seems to have just returned from a night out. With neat dramatic irony the dog, unseen by the characters in the print, draws our attention to a young woman's cap in his master's pocket, which indicates how the young lord has been spending his time.

To re-inforce these factual and narrative elements, Hogarth uses details of the furnishing and decoration of the rooms to echo and symbolise the state of the couple's marriage. The lack of harmony between them is reflected everywhere, from the mixture of Chinese and Indian statuettes and bottles surrounding the Roman bust on the mantelpiece, to the hilarious mixture of inappropriate figures nestling in the rococo clock above the husband's head. A more straightforward indication of the couple's lack of affection is shown by the painting of Cupid behind the Roman bust, his bow unstrung, surrounded by ruins. The point is re-inforced by the paintings on the wall of the adjoining room; hung immediately adjacent to four full-length figures of male saints is an erotic image apparently so shocking that it has to be covered by a curtain.

Hogarth began advertising the *Marriage à-la-Mode* prints about two years before they were actually published. This was done partly to gain time to collect as many subscription orders as possible; anyone subscribing in advance of publication would pay only the reduced price of one guinea for the set, whereas after publication the price rose to 1½ guineas. In this way Hogarth could gather money towards the initial costs of materials (paper, copper plates, etc), hiring engravers, and paying printers before actually starting on the project. He chose to employ French engravers since they were generally thought to be the only ones capable of producing work sufficiently skilled and sophisticated to attract the kind of purchaser he had in mind—purchasers from the very class to be satirized in the plates. The composition of the images, however, was entirely Hogarth's work; he executed a series of six oil paintings (now in the National Gallery, London) from which the engravers were to work. The paintings, displayed in Hogarth's studio, encouraged subscribers to order copies of the prints but, surprisingly, although his prints sold well enough, Hogarth often had great difficulty in selling the original paintings; the *Marriage à-la-Mode* series was eventually auctioned in 1751. Clearly Hogarth's contemporaries felt that, whereas this kind of social satire may be acceptable in the form of prints, it completely failed to meet the requirements of the more elevated medium of oil paint.   SH

Invented Painted & Published by Wm Hogarth.

Marriage-A-la-Mode. (Plate II)

Engraved by B. Baron.

According to Act of Parliament April 1st 1745.

The Lion Bas-Reliefs 1761

Plate V from Carceri d'Invenzione (Imaginary Prisons)
Designed and etched by Giovanni Battista Piranesi (1720-1778) Italian

Etching with engraving; second state of three; plate mark 560 x 412 mm

Presented through the Friends of the Whitworth by M.K. Burrows in 1954 (5763)

The set of prints from which this etching is taken, *Carceri d'Invenzione* (Imaginary Prisons) has an intriguing history. The series was first published around 1749-50 as a set of fourteen plates. Over ten years later, Piranesi took up the copper plates again and substantially re-worked most of the images, as well as adding two completely new plates, one of which is shown opposite. Much had happened to Piranesi during the intervening years. He had come to Rome from Venice in 1740, mainly to study the remains of ancient Roman architecture; by 1760 he was known internationally for his publications, containing plans, maps, elevations and sections of the magnificent buildings of Rome, as well as reconstructions of the engineering methods used in their construction. These clearly established Piranesi as the foremost artistic proponent of Roman architecture, defending its originality against growing opposition from a group of scholars claiming that Roman architects merely learned their skills from Greek examples.

The ideas which had preoccupied Piranesi during the 1750s help to explain why, at the end of the decade, he should want to re-work a set of prints of imaginary architecture such as the *Carceri*. As they first appeared, most of the images did not look much like prisons; certainly their spacious expanses were quite unlike the tiny, claustrophobic prison cells that Piranesi might have seen in contemporary Venice or Rome. Piranesi's title stressed, however, that these were 'imaginary' prisons, and it must have been the freedom which the subject gave him to invent vast, simple architectural structures that initially attracted him.

But, when he came to re-work the plates, Piranesi's ideas had changed. As he etched more lines to clarify the structure of the buildings, the images became darker; as he added more objects, including, in various places, sharply pointed iron spikes, the scenes took on an oppressive air of menace. But Piranesi also made alterations which would seem to contradict this effect— he expanded the background spaces of many of the compositions by adding more ranges of arches leading to open spaces and this clearly went against the supposed restraining functions of the buildings. The plate illustrated opposite, though newly invented for the second edition, has all the characteristics of the altered plates: the clutter of objects and the ominously spiked beams, as well as the sense of lightness and airiness given by the view through the archways to the right.

The art historian Andrew Robison has argued that the main clue to the interpretation of these new plates lies in the figures. Despite their lively poses and expressions, the huge ones to the left are clearly ancient stone bas-reliefs. The armed captors in military helmets are escorting captives, bound and chained. All the other figures are much smaller and, unlike the more classically draped stone figures, they are dressed in the costume of Piranesi's Roman contemporaries. These smaller figures wander freely about, staring or gesticulating at the structure towering above them. It seems clear that, unlike his earlier, more generalised imaginary prisons, this later etching shows the remains of an ancient Roman prison, demonstrating the harshness of ancient Roman justice, whilst the simple magnificence of their buildings inspires admiration and wonder in the Romans of Piranesi's time.

In his theoretical treatises, such as *Antichità Romane...* of 1756, Piranesi had praised the simple, monumental structures of the early, heroic period of Roman architecture. He claimed that their huge hewn stones and unadorned monumental arches were characteristics which provided evidence that Roman civilization had evolved independently from Greece, their architecture deriving instead from the work of the Etruscans. He presented his theories in a factual manner, but they understandably affected the re-working of his more imaginative etchings, so that the new *Carceri d'Invenzione* became more solemn images, conveying not only the grand, overpowering magnificence of the architecture of the ancient Romans, but also the harshness of their laws and the severity of their punishments. SH

Figures at a Well 1763

Hubert Robert (1733-1808) French

Red chalk 392 x 542 mm

Purchased in 1960 with the aid of a grant from the
Victoria and Albert Museum Purchase Grant Fund (D.8.1960)

Robert executed this drawing in Italy in 1763 towards the end of an eleven year stay in Rome which constituted the bulk of his education as an artist. Previously Robert, who came from a well-off middle class family in Paris, had been a pupil of the sculptor Rene-Michel Slodtz, but like most ambitious young artists of the day his immediate goal was a place at the French Academy at Rome. The Academy had been established by Louis XIV in 1666 in order to allow French artists to study the masterpieces of the past, both classical and the more recent works of Raphael and the Carracci, with the aim of producing a national school of French History painters to rival the Italians. Each year young artists competed for the coveted Prix de Rome, an award which effectively guaranteed an artist's future. Robert did not win but instead was fortunate to be invited by his father's former employer, the Comte de Stainville, who had just been appointed Ambassador to the Pope, to accompany him to Rome. It was de Stainville who arranged for Robert to attend the Academy; after five years he was finally accepted as a 'pensionnaire' and went on to complete the three year course.

Robert was fortunate in that his stay in Rome coincided with the directorship of the Academy of Charles-Joseph Natoire who, as a balance to the rather dry traditional curriculum of life study and copying from casts, encouraged the students to sketch directly from nature. Academic theory still regarded landscape as being inferior to History painting (subjects taken from the Bible and from the classics) but in Rome and in the surrounding countryside (the Campagna) landscape was thought to have, through associations with the past, an elevating quality. Robert, like many of his contemporaries in Rome, was particularly interested in the ruins of antiquity and following the example of the Italian artists Panini and Piranesi (see p.44) was able to develop a type of landscape, the antique ruin, which married a traditional concern for classical culture with a growing interest in landscape for its own sake. Mindful therefore of his future career as a painter in oils of 'ruin pieces', Robert produced numerous sketches executed swiftly on the spot which could act as a storehouse of images as well as a topographical record of sites. What started out for Robert as a study exercise quickly became of more direct practical use.

Robert did not limit himself to simple topographical views but, like Panini and Canaletto, he also produced what are called 'Capriccios', mixtures of real and imaginary buildings assembled by the artist. This particular scene has not been identified and, although it does not necessarily mean that it falls into the category of invention, there are a number of features which suggest at least some of the scene comes from the artist's imagination. Firstly the figure of the washerwoman, and the horse drinking, are very close to figures in a number of other drawings and suggest that they are part of a set of types. Figures, though usually small in scale, play an important part in ruin scenes, emphasising the moral of the decline of a once great empire or, as in this case, adding a pleasing picturesque element which underlines the sense of harmony between man and nature. The second point is that the size of the drawing, the signature and the date (hidden amongst the steps), suggests that the artist may well have had a purchaser in mind. By 1763 Robert had begun to build up a circle of patrons some of whom may have been able to appreciate the marvellous range of textural effects which the artist was able to achieve using the red chalk medium. The technique of the drawing clearly indicates that it was sketched very quickly, something that is often associated with working out of doors; what we probably have in this case is therefore a study from nature which is rather more than a simple record of a place and event and which was more than utilitarian in purpose. GS

The Island of the Madonna del Monte in the Venetian Lagoon c1779

Francesco Tironi (c1745-1797) Italian

Brown pen and grey wash with bodycolour, over red chalk underdrawing 280 x 420 mm

Purchased in 1922 (D.3.1922)

This drawing by the little known Venetian artist Francesco Tironi was made to be reproduced as an etching. It was published in 1779, along with twenty three others, as *Isole della Laguna* (Islands of the Lagoon). The publisher, Teodoro Viero, a well known printer and printseller, hoped to tap the demand for topographical views of Venice and its environs and produce an attractive souvenir for the visitors who flocked to the city every year. The publication concentrated on some of the many picturesque islands which surround Venice and on the trade and water traffic of the Lagoon. This view, which was number twenty-three in the sequence, shows the tiny island of Madonna del Monte with the church of Saint Catherine dominating the scene. Unlike Canaletto, who in the 1740s had produced a number of topographical etchings himself, Tironi executed the drawings for another, Antonio Sandi, to copy. The etcher added seven birds to, what is otherwise, a remarkably faithful copy of the Whitworth drawing, in a medium which was only rarely used for reproductions.

The drawing was bought by the Gallery in 1922 as a Canaletto and it was only in 1960 that the current attribution was accepted. Given the inscription on the print there is no doubt that the drawing is by Tironi. As one of only a handful of works definitely by Tironi it is thus of the greatest significance and helps us to reconstruct the career of this enigmatic artist. With the benefit of hindsight it now seems odd that it could ever have been considered to be by Canaletto; apart from the subject matter there are few or no stylistic links between the two artists; indeed Canaletto died ten years before the drawing was executed. One source of confusion was the inscription on the back: *N.1001 A.Canaletto* which was added at some point in the past by a collector or dealer. There is no reason, however, to believe that this inscription was added to confuse or to increase the financial value of the drawing, though it is possible; rather it is entirely typical of the way in which unsigned works by minor artists become, with the passing of time, attributed to their more famous contemporaries. In many cases this has meant that followers, students and later copyists have completely clouded our image of an artist, whilst a mass of secondary figures, whom we may know only from documentary sources, are lost from view.

The continuing process of refining and paring down the number of works attributed to the famous is the less spectacular side of the connoisseur tradition which is represented in the press by the rarer occurrence of a 'discovery'. Certainly this has helped to foster a popular misconception that there are 'masterpieces' waiting to be recognised in the vaults and basements of our public galleries. More often than not, and this drawing is a good case in point, it is the removal of works attributed to a famous name that increases our knowledge of a period. If one looks at old Whitworth catalogues we have 'lost' quite a few 'Constables', 'Turners' over the years.

Tironi provides a good example of that strange phenomenon, a 'rediscovered artist'. Again it is a myth (the discovery of a lost or unrecognised genius), which clouds the more prosaic reality that rediscovery generally means understanding more about the typical competent professionals of a given period. In the case of Tironi the quality of the drawing is very high but, not untypically, in spite of every effort, we still know remarkably little about him. His birth date is unknown and, although he is recorded as having been a painter, none of his paintings has been conclusively identified. Various dictionaries of artists record that he was a priest, which may account for the scarcity of his work, but it is still possible that a lifetime's work is waiting to be recognised. GS

Wallpaper and border

Wallpaper attributed to the Studio of Jean-Baptiste Reveillon French, c1789

Border manufactured by Jacquemart & Bénard, c1795
Portion of hand-printed wallpaper and border, colour print from wood blocks 600 x 1030 mm

Purchased in 1986 with the aid of a grant from the
Victoria and Albert Museum Purchase Grant Fund (W.13.1986)

By 1800, thanks to the efforts of manufacturers such as Jean-Baptiste Reveillon, the art of colour printing with wood blocks had been 'brought to perfection'. The available range of wall hangings had widened considerably since the beginning of the century, when only the very best flock papers could compete with Chinese hand painted decorations.

It was the mid-eighteenth-century fashion for flocked and distemper printed wallpapers from England that gave the Paris shopkeeper Reveillon an opportunity to exercise his entrepreneurial flair in the wallpaper trade. Credited with being the first to hang English papers properly, he imported and retailed them, advertising that he had a large quantity of "real English flock hangings imitating Persian hangings, Utrecht velvets and damasks". Within a few years he was manufacturing his own ranges and, in the early 1760s, re-located his factory in a mansion in the Faubourg Saint Antoine, the paper-staining centre of Paris. By the late 1780s he had purchased and re-organised a paper mill at Courtalin, and had been awarded the title of royal warrant holder, which gave him permission to "engrave, colour, print, paint, flock and sell wholesale or retail all sorts of paper, card, stuff, textile, leather or skin". He was employing more than three hundred people.

The artistic and technical expertise of his factory was brought to the attention of a vast audience when, thanks to an arrangement with the Montgolfier brothers, a huge balloon, seventy feet high with twenty-four bands of Reveillon's printed paper affixed, soared above Versailles in September 1784.

His manufacturing operation was a model of proto-industrialisation, with a division of labour which anticipated nineteenth-century mass production. Further, by retaining control over both production and marketing as well as the manufacture of the raw materials, he was able to maintain high standards of quality control. In addition, his awareness that the success of his enterprise depended to a large extent on the skill of his designers and technicians led him to employ fashionable decorative artists,

and, as design copyright did not exist in France before 1793, to copy the styles of many others.

Reveillon's output was large and varied and included flocked papers, said to be "among the most beautiful ever produced in France", copies of Indian cotton and Lyons silk designs, 'perfect' imitations of both toiles de Jouy designs and Jean Pillement's chinoiserie styles. However, he is most famous for the neo-classical designs he began to produce after 1780. Many were in the style of the artist Jean-Baptiste Fay, who specialised in the imitation of Pompeian wall-paintings and who may have worked for Reveillon between 1775-89. These designs were produced as panels, and provided a cheaper alternative to painted decorations, and the fact that they were integrated with the interiors of large houses and châteaux stimulated the demand for the printed paper hangings. Featuring arabesques, floral garlands and bouquets, and adorned with birds, beasts, and insects, the panels often incorporated plaques, roundels and other architectural devices and were frequently more than eight feet high. Occasionally, chinoiserie motifs were used but these were more frequently employed in repeating patterns, such as the example illustrated here, which contains both the chinoiserie elements and the arrangements of exotic flora typical of the pseudo-Chinese styles fashionable in Europe during the latter part of the eighteenth century. The combination of brilliant, pure colours, in particular the use of intense orange, is characteristic of Reveillon's productions.

A flamboyant character, Reveillon thrived on publicity and it was perhaps a combination of envy at his success together with the collapse of the social order which provided the market for his luxury products that led to his downfall. In 1789 his factory was burnt by a revolutionary mob and, disillusioned, he left for England, disposing of what remained of the business to Jacquemart and Bénard. Ironically, this firm subsequently produced a number of designs which incorporated revolutionary motifs.   CW

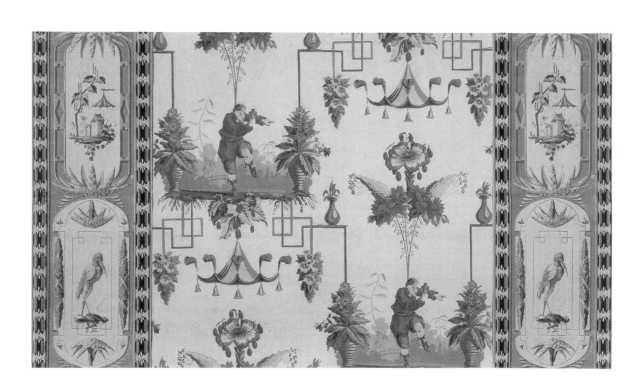

Bird and Flower

China: 18th century

Portion of hand-painted wallpaper, tempera 2565 x 914 mm
Presented by the Wall Paper Manufacturers Ltd in 1967 (W.112.1967)

Towards the end of the seventeenth century, Chinese decorated papers began to arrive in Europe, initially with Dutch traders and later via the East India Company. Wallpapers were rarely used in Chinese homes. The painted decorations which became fashionable in European interiors during the eighteenth century were produced solely for export, and probably inspired by Oriental silk hangings. As their popularity increased these exotic, brightly coloured papers were rapidly adapted to suit western tastes and, by mid-century, had become a feature of rooms which also incorporated Chinese pictures, toys, lacquerware, and other 'choicest movables of China'. The vogue for Chinese papers became such that Cantonese merchants began to export them in sets of 25-40 rolls, each roll made up of several sheets pasted together, and with a number to indicate the sequence in which they should be hung. Spare rolls were often supplied in order that extra motifs—birds, branches, etc—could be cut out and stuck on, both to disguise the joins and provide added interest. These papers contained no repeating patterns and, as they did not follow the conventions of western perspective, they created a seamless pattern of colour and movement around the room. The range of subjects and motifs was limited and falls into three groups.

The first shows scenes of industry and daily life and tends to be dominated by human figures. A set of papers in this style covering an area thirty feet long by twenty feet broad was brought to England around 1792 by the first British Ambassador to Pekin. It depicts a whole variety of activities, such as the processes of rice and tea cultivation, and has some three hundred figures. That these scenes were realistically depicted was verified by the botanist, Sir Joseph Banks, who commented in 1770 that "A man need go no further to study the Chinese than the China paper, the better sorts of which represent their persons and such of their customs, dress, etc, as I have seen, most strikingly like".

The second, more common group of papers, features flowering plants, birds, and insects and Banks was also impressed with the accuracy of the botanical detail of these. The designs usually comprise flowering trees, which climb the length of the paper from rocky pools or sandy ground, and they have birds and insects fluttering or perched amidst the foliage. Occasionally, low ornamental balustrades, potted shrubs, lanterns, and other details enliven the foreground, and bird-cages are suspended from the branches.

The third group of papers combines elements from the other two, having flowering trees filling the top three-quarters whilst scenes of domestic life crowd the lower section. It is probable that these papers were produced in response to demand from Europe and date from the second half of the eighteenth century.

The designs were applied by hand; first the outline in black ink, and then the flat colour. Details were applied last and, in some cases, the flowers and fruit had coloured glazes. The example shown here belongs to the bird and flower group, the most characteristic of Chinese productions as a whole, and is one of a set, probably of twenty-five rolls. It incorporates the motifs usually associated with this group: blossoming trees with slender meandering branches, camellias, peonies and pomegranates; doves, partridges, peacocks, etc, perch on a rocky formation at the base, and smaller birds and butterflies are in flight amongst the branches. Two of the birds have been cut from another piece and pasted on.

There are signs that, at some stage in its history, the paper has been used as part of a decorative scheme. Unlike most later wallpapers, these Chinese decorations were not attached directly to the wall but were nailed to a canvas backing stretched over a wooden framework. By this means they were protected from damp walls and it is to this unusual method of paper hanging that we owe the survival of these fragile decorations.   CW

The Stud Farm 1786
Thomas Rowlandson (1756-1827) British

Watercolour and pen and ink over pencil 275 x 388mm

Presented by A.E. Anderson in 1934 (D.25.1934)

Thomas Rowlandson, a true Londoner, was the son of a City merchant and, later in life, the recorder of innumerable London scenes and events. After training at the Royal Academy Schools and completing his studies in Paris, Rowlandson started to exhibit his work at the Royal Academy in 1775, and became a regular contributor there until 1787, first showing portrait drawings and then humorous genre subjects and caricatures, for which he is now best known. He worked mainly in pen and watercolour over pencil and was undoubtedly one of the most skilful and gifted draughtsmen of the late Georgian period. Rowlandson was not averse to exposing or ridiculing the antics of high society in London—the Duchess of Devonshire at the gaming tables and canvassing for Charles James Fox, the scramble of *cognoscenti* on the staircase of the Royal Academy and gross dowagers parading at a St James' Palace reception. However, other subjects are depicted in a kinder mood and there is considerable gaiety and charm in scenes like *Skating on the Serpentine* and *Vauxhall Gardens,* 1784.

Although Rowlandson's name tends to be more frequently associated with the portrayal of the coarser side of life, and his characters are frequently crude and offensive, he had a genuine love for the country, which was expressed in his gentler watercolours of landscape compositions and country pursuits. Throughout the eighteenth century, sporting pictures were immensely popular with British patrons and collectors. John Wootton received numerous commissions in the first half of the century for portraits of horses, park landscapes with hunting scenes, and conversation pieces with equestrian figures. The greatest exponent of this type of painting flourished in the second half of the century when George Stubbs produced masterpieces brilliantly composed around the frieze motif including the Duke of Grafton's *Mares and Foals by a Stream* and the Tate Gallery's *Mares and Foals in a River Landscape.* Rowlandson is not usually thought of in this context, but in his *Stud Farm* he chose the same type of subject, resulting in a composition closely related to the above paintings, though executed in watercolour. The outdoor activities of the English gentry were often recorded in his work and his style was well suited to the lively atmosphere and the bustle of the characters in the set of six fox-hunting scenes of 1787, in the J.Leslie Wright collection in Birmingham City Art Gallery. Other watercolours were devoted to pure landscapes, his trees being distinguished by their free handling and Rococo mannerisms. Gainsborough's influence is strong in a number of them, for example *A Country Scene with Peasants at a Cottage Door,* Boston Public Library, U.S.A.

The Stud Farm is not entirely unique in Rowlandson's *oeuvre* for there are several other drawings of similar groups of horses—*Horses grouped round an Oak Tree,* c.1795-1800, in the National Gallery of Canada, Ottowa, *Horses beneath a Tree,* in the Ashmolean Museum, Oxford, and various studies in the Paul Mellon collection. *The Duke of Grafton viewing his Stud* shows the mounted nobleman on one side staring intently at his stud in an open field on the other side of a gate, while *The Horse Fair* in the Victoria and Albert Museum is slightly different in theme, in that it is a much more ambitious and crowded composition in the setting of a large square bordered by village church and inn.

FWH

Richard Payne Knight c1793-4

Sir Thomas Lawrence (1769-1830) British

Oil on canvas 1270 x 1015 mm

Presented by Her Majesty's Treasury in 1975 (O.2.1975)

Thomas Lawrence's portrait of Richard Payne Knight is very different from the standard image of the gentleman scholar, but then Payne Knight was far from being a typical amateur intellectual. The portrait convention for the scholar, seated in his library and surrounded by his treasures and suitable reminders of his illustrious predecessors, had been established in the Middle Ages and had survived to be transformed, in the hands of artists like Joshua Reynolds, into a staple image associated with the English Gentleman. In portrait after portrait during the eighteenth century of gentlemen in their libraries, or seen against a Grand Tour backdrop, the attainment of learning was shown to be as natural, and as easily acquired, as the ownership of land and the exercising of power; and it was worn with the same air of nonchalant detachment. Not surprisingly, this startling image provoked one critic, on the occasion of its showing at the Royal Academy in 1794, to exclaim "It fills me with the idea of an irascible pedagogue explaining euclid to a dunce... This is surely the saturnalia of vice and insignificance!" Instead of the sensitive aesthete carefully handling a beautiful object from his collection we have an image of a corpulent, lascivious man interrupted by a sudden thought or shaft of inspiration as he manhandles a great tome; meanwhile, and as a joke which must have been sanctioned by the sitter, a bronze vase from his collection with handles in the form of figures appears ready to pounce on him.

As was the convention of the day the portrait was listed in the catalogue of the Royal Academy only as "a portrait of a gentleman"; but few of the, by today's standards, small audience who visited the Academy, would have been unaware of the sitter's identity. Payne Knight had already made a considerable reputation for himself as a scholar and a collector. His tours on the Continent in the years 1772-3 and 1777 had revealed the riches of the classical tradition and he responded with a number of publications, including the notorious *Account of the Worship of Priapus* and the *Analytical Essay on the Greek Alphabet*. By 1794 he had also completed the remodelling of his family home,

Downton Castle. Many of the principles used at Downton and in the laying out of the grounds were to be elucidated in *The Landscape—A Didactic Poem* published in 1794. In particular the poem sought to express Knight's opposition to the style of landscape gardening popularised by 'Capability Brown'. He supported instead the cause of the Picturesque, a term used to characterise an aesthetic category, not covered by the Sublime or the Beautiful, and which might be summarised as the capacity to please through a combination of a roughness and irregularity of form and a series of venerable associations. Payne Knight developed his ideas on the Picturesque in his *Analytical Inquiry Into the Principles of Taste* and, in a career which increasingly included public controversy, was established as one of the most influential thinkers and arbiters of taste of the day.

It is important to establish Payne Knight's academic credentials in order to understand how unconventional this image must have appeared. It is not just that Lawrence refused to flatter Payne Knight—he actually makes a positive attempt to reinforce the sitter's arrogance and eccentricity. In achieving this Lawrence refers to another portrait convention associated with the scholar, that of the Evangelist portrait where the writer of the Gospels, or other holy writings is shown receiving divine inspiration from an angel or a dove representing the Holy Spirit. The portrait recalls representations of St John composing his Gospel such as Titian's painting in the church of S.Maria della Salute in Venice and this must have troubled an audience aware of Payne Knight's reputation. One needs to emphasise that this was painted as a commission and that Payne Knight paid for the work and that it hung over the fireplace in his library where it remained for almost two hundred years until its acquisition by the Whitworth. Its exhibition at the Royal Academy was not to sell the work but to demonstrate the artist's skill, and to keep his name in the public eye. In allowing his property to be exhibited Payne Knight further underlined his complicity in the promotion of a flamboyant public image. GS

The Lake of Nemi looking towards Genzano c1777

John Robert Cozens (1752-1797) British

Watercolour 360 x 528mm

Presented by J.E. Taylor in 1892 (D.24.1892)

John Robert Cozens was the son of the watercolourist and art master Alexander, from whom he learnt the rudiments of drawing and methods of landscape composition. Cozens went twice to Italy, the first occasion being 1776 when his visit was under the patronage of Richard Payne Knight (see p.56), connoisseur and collector of bronzes, drawings and other works of art. He stayed there for three years, basing himself in Rome but making expeditions across the Campagna to the Alban Hills. His second trip took place in 1782-3, as draughtsman to the extremely rich and eccentric William Beckford, for whom he completed a series of watercolours of Italian landscapes. The seven sketchbooks which Cozens filled on this second tour were acquired for the Whitworth in 1975. Many of his finest watercolours over the following ten years were derived from the pen and grey wash studies in these books but by 1794, Cozens was mentally ill and he was placed under the medical care of Dr Thomas Monro for the last few years of his life.

On his trip of 1776-79, Cozens worked mainly in Rome, where he became interested in some of the great classical monuments and produced watercolours of the Castel S. Angelo and the Colosseum, reminiscent of some of G.B. Piranesi's designs. In April 1777 he was sketching around Tivoli and the area of Lake Albano and Lake Nemi, according to dated inscriptions on some of the drawings in the volume of *28 Sketches by J. Cozens of Views in Italy, 1776-78* in the Sir John Soane Museum, London. This view of Lake Nemi and the small town of Genzano, on the south-west rim of its crater, is based on a rough sketch in the Soane Museum volume. Inscribed *Gensano*, it is take from the grounds of the Capuchin monastery, situated in an elevated position slightly to the north, and surrounded by gardens of pine and cypress trees. A similar view of Genzano was drawn by Richard Wilson for William Legge, 2nd Earl of Dartmouth, in 1754, and the Whitworth owns a watercolour of the same subject by Thomas Jones, dated 8th May, 1777.

The central area of this tranquil scene is dominated by the precarious and irregular slope of the crater, surmounted by the cluster of buildings around Palazzo Cesarini. In the Soane Museum sketch, the artist gives a far more gentle incline to the cliff, and the palace itself is less conspicuous. Balanced on either side of this central feature are the extensive plain reaching to the sea and Monte Circeo on the left, and a wooded foreground on the right with the trees much reduced in scale and height from those shown in the original pencil sketch. As was often the case in Cozens' work when a subject proved popular with collectors, this view was repeated by him a number of times, at least six other versions being known, including two in the British Museum, one at Stourhead, and another in the Whitworth's collection.

There are two pencil and grey wash studies of the promontory of Monte Circeo in Cozens' Grand Tour sketchbooks, one dated 5th July 1782 in Volume I, when William Beckford and his party were on their way from Rome to Naples, and the other 9th December 1782 in Volume V, when the artist was travelling back to Rome on his own.

The Soane Museum's book contains two other drawings of Lake Nemi, both of which served as preliminary studies for watercolours. Other sketches in the book include views of Lake Albano, Tivoli, and the Campagna. These studies were used by Cozens as the basis of large watercolours for the remainder of his working life, and even in his last phase he was still able to express his highly personal feelings for the atmosphere and poetic mood of the Italian landscape. His influence on the early development of the young Thomas Girtin and J.M.W. Turner was considerable and his work was particularly admired by John Constable in whose opinion "Cousins was all poetry". FWH

Durham Cathedral and Bridge, from the River Wear 1799

Thomas Girtin (1775-1802) British

Watercolour with faint pencil and scratching out 416 x 537mm

Presented by J.E. Taylor in 1892 (D.110.1892)

Thomas Girtin was born in Southwark only two months earlier than Turner. Contemporary documentation about his life is scarce, though he is known to have been apprenticed in 1788 to the topographical watercolourist Edward Dayes, from whom he learnt the method of the tinted drawing by filling in outlines with grey-blue washes and then adding touches of colour. There is a strong influence of Dayes' style in the earliest works of Girtin, but some disagreement between master and pupil was apparently responsible for the apprenticeship being reduced to three years. Dayes was piqued about this, and wrote posthumously of Girtin in *Professional Sketches of Modern Artists*, 1805: "Though his drawings are generally too slight, yet they must ever be admired as the offspring of a strong imagination. Had he not trifled away a vigorous constitution, he might have arrived at a very high degree of excellence as a landscape painter."

Girtin accompanied the antiquarian publisher James Moore on a tour of the Midlands in 1794 and the pencil sketches which he made on that journey were the basis for some of the artist's finest early watercolours, like his views of the west fronts of Lichfield and Peterborough Cathedrals. In the same year, 1794, Girtin showed for the first time at the Royal Academy and he continued to exhibit there until 1801. It was about this time that he and Turner first visited Dr Thomas Monro's house in the Adelphi. Joseph Farington noted in his *Diary*; "Turner and Girtin told us they had been employed by Dr Monro 3 years to draw at his house in the evenings. They went at 6 and staid till Tea. Girtin drew in outlines and Turner washed in the effects. They were chiefly employed in copying the outlines or unfinished drawings of Cozens, &c &c of which Copies they made finished drawings" (12th November 1798).

The view of the three towers of Durham Cathedral in their commanding position above the River Wear inspired many landscape artists in the late eighteenth and nineteenth centuries, and Thomas Hearne, Edward Dayes, Turner and Cotman were among the other watercolourists who recorded the scene. Girtin went to the North of England and Scottish Border country for the first time in 1796 and this watercolour of Durham is based on a pencil study of the Cathedral viewed from the north, made on that occasion and now in the Museum of Fine Arts, Boston. Both the original sketch and a smaller watercolour version of the view show the corner of a building at the extreme right of the composition, but this has been omitted from the Whitworth's watercolour; otherwise it follows the main outlines of the original sketch very closely.

Durham Cathedral and Bridge, from the River Wear is one of Girtin's most impressive compositions. The monumental structure of Framwellgate Bridge provides a strong horizontal base for the massive forms of the castle and Cathedral above it. By the time that the artist produced this version of 1799, he had perfected his mastery of architectural draughtsmanship by copying works by Thomas Malton the Younger, Piranesi, Marco Ricci and Canaletto. There is still a strong hint of Canaletto in the watercolour, both in the treatment of architectural detail and in the activities of the various figures along the bank and in the punt.

Between 1795 and 1799 Girtin produced several other studies of Durham Cathedral, including a watercolour after Dayes in the Laing Art Gallery, Newcastle-upon-Tyne, and another in the Victoria and Albert Museum, both views being taken from the north. There are two further watercolours, showing the building from the south-west.

FWH

The Chapter House, Salisbury Cathedral c1799

Joseph Mallord William Turner (1775-1851) British

Watercolour and pen and ink over pencil 645 x 512mm

Presented by Sir William Agnew in 1891 (D.3.1889)

Turner, "the only perfect landscape painter whom the world has ever seen" according to John Ruskin, was born in the same year as Girtin at Covent Garden, London, the son of a barber and wig-maker. Entering the Royal Academy Schools in 1789, he received early training in perspective drawing under Thomas Malton the Younger. He was still a teenager when he first exhibited at the Royal Academy in 1790, and he was to remain a regular exhibitor there throughout his life, becoming an Associate in 1799 and a full Academician in 1802. It was around 1794 when Turner and the young Thomas Girtin started to study Dr Thomas Monro's collection in the Adelphi and were paid by him to copy the sketches and watercolours of John Robert Cozens.

Turner was to be an inveterate traveller all his life and he filled his sketchbooks on each journey with landscape drawings, outlines of buildings, and colour notes and sketches. Most of these are now in the Clore Gallery at the Tate Gallery, London. Turner's first Midlands Tour was in 1794 when he visited Warwick, Peterborough and Ely, and in the following year, he travelled to the Isle of Wight, stopping at Salisbury to make sketches of the Cathedral. In 1796 he exhibited a watercolour of *The Close Gate, Salisbury* at the Royal Academy, and this was followed by six Salisbury Cathedral subjects, shown there between 1797 and 1801. These were part of a set of Salisbury views commissioned by Sir Richard Colt Hoare of Stourhead, as illustrations for his history of Wiltshire, but they were never used. By the time that he commenced work on the series, Turner had already shown a brilliant gift for architectural draughtsmanship in works like *St Anselm's Chapel, Canterbury*, 1794, and the west front of Peterborough, 1795. In the Isle of Wight sketchbook, 1795, he listed two Salisbury subjects, *Salisbury Porch* and *Front of Salisbury*, with Sir Richard Hoare's name written alongside them and, later in the same book, there are sketches of *The West Front* and *Part of the Exterior of the Cathedral*. He appears to have completed eight different views for Hoare and these are noted in one of his other sketchbooks as *2 Chapter. 2 inside. 1 Cloyster. 2 outside. 1 general*. The Royal Academy exhibits were *The Choir with Lady Chapel*, 1797 (untraced), the *Inside of the Chapter House*, 1799, *The West Front*, 1799 (Harris Museum, Preston), and *Chapter House*, 1801 (Victoria and Albert Museum). The three additional subjects owned by Hoare were *View of the Cathedral from the Bishop's Garden*, c.1797-8, in the Birmingham City Art Gallery, the dramatic *South View from the Cloisters*, c.1802, in the Victoria and Albert Museum, and *Interior looking towards the North Transept*, 1802-5, in the Salisbury and South Wiltshire Museum.

Around the same period, the artist completed a number of watercolours of other church interiors, the most striking being the British Museum's *Interior of Westminster Abbey*, various views inside Ely Cathedral, and the *Transept of Ewenny Priory*, in the National Museum of Wales. He had benefited greatly from his training in architectural topography and perspective under Malton, and the influence of Edward Dayes on his work in the early 1790s was equally important. The scale of the Ely and Salisbury Cathedral interiors is ambitious, and the dramatic boldness of his compositions and their astonishing inventiveness are comparable to similar qualities in the outstanding architectural *capricci* of Piranesi. Other leading watercolourists in the late 18th century had also come under Piranesi's spell, like J.R. Cozens in his watercolours of the Colosseum, 1778, and Girtin, who copied several Piranesi subjects. Turner achieved the same imaginative power and technical skills in his treatment of massive architectural forms and heightened the drama of each scene with spectacular light and shade effects.   FWH

Tiger Hunting Scene 1815

Produced by Dufour et Cie

Wallpaper, colour print from wood blocks 2286 x 1600mm

Presented by the Wall Paper Manufacturers Limited in 1967 (W.176i.1967)

The *Tiger Hunting Scene* consists of three panels from the scenic decoration *Les Vues de L'Inde*, and is one of a small but highly influential group of wallpapers that were produced in France during the first half of the nineteenth century. Unlike most other wallpapers of this period which had small, floral or ornamental repeats, scenic decorations contained large, non-repeating pictorial designs that formed a panoramic scene running continuously around the room. Contemporaries compared them to fine art and their use of devices such as perspective and modelling to create an impression of space and depth does indeed seem more indebted to mural painting than to wallpaper design. Today such illusionism may appear somewhat inappropriate in a decoration for a flat and solid surface like a wall. It acts, however, as a reminder of the heights to which the industry aspired and the artistry, craftsmanship and sheer spectacle of such wallpapers cannot be denied.

Scenic decorations first appeared in 1804 and *Les Vues de L'Inde* therefore represents quite an early example of the genre. It was produced in 1815 by Dufour et Cie, a Parisian firm based in the Faubourg Saint-Antoine. Scenic decorations constituted a new departure for the company: the majority of their work had previously consisted mainly of expensive, hand-printed patterns imitating silks, draperies, and classical grisailles. Nevertheless, they became an increasingly important part of the firm's *oeuvre* and did much to establish Dufour et Cie as the foremost manufacturer of the period.

The *Tiger Hunting Scene* was the fifth of Dufour's scenic designs. However, its colourful depiction of native peoples in a foreign land was characteristic of previous and later scenic themes. Similar incidents had been portrayed in *Les Sauvages de la Mer Pacifique* of c.1806 while parts of the landscape were adapted for *Les Paysages de Telemaque* which was issued c.1825. This repetition did not simply reflect a lack of inventiveness on the manufacturer's part but was also a calculated response to the growing popularity of such themes. Public interest in primitive cultures had originally been awakened in the 1760s and 1770s with

the reports of voyagers such as Captain Cook. By the early 1800s their curiosity knew no bounds. Decorations like *Les Vues de L'Inde* appealed to an audience hungry for knowledge of exotic climes and its fanciful portrayal of unfamiliar peoples and lands confirmed a belief in the picturesqueness and nobility of 'uncivilised' races that was widespread at the time. Dufour's work has also been related to the aquatints of William Daniell, published in his *Oriental Scenery* of 1779. The Indian temples and villages that appear in other panels of *Les Vues de L'Inde* (W.176ii-iii.1967) are indeed similar to those represented in Daniell's work but the dramatic action and bold design of the *Tiger Hunting Scene* may be more profitably compared to the Romantic paintings of George Stubbs or Carl Van Loo.

Scenic decorations were extremely time-consuming and therefore costly to produce. Recent historians have estimated that the total length of time needed to research, prepare and print a set of designs could be as long as eighteen months to two years. Even so, the more ambitious manufacturers were not deterred and a surprisingly large number of different decorations were produced. They were sold to middle and upper class homes whose owners were assured of the didactic value of the different themes. Dufour, for example, claimed that the botanical details in a decoration such as *Les Vues de L'Inde* could serve a useful function in the education of the young: "The mother of a family will give history and geography lessons to a lively little girl. The several kinds of vegetation can themselves serve as an introduction to the history of plants". Even a more disinterested observer remarked that scenic decorations could be "a useful encyclopaedia to study while waiting for the soup", though Theophile Gautier's comments were perhaps, in this instance, more sardonic than sincere. For most customers, however, it was the colour, beauty and novelty of scenic designs that appealed: and they constituted fascinating and fashionable alternatives to the more conventional and expensive mural painting and tapestries. JB

The Ancient of Days c1824
William Blake (1757-1827) British

Watercolour, bodycolour, black ink and gold paint over
a relief etched outline printed in yellow 234 x 168mm

Presented by J.E. Taylor in 1892 (D.32.1892)

One of the leading figurative illustrators and poets of the Romantic period, William Blake was born in London, where he spent most of his life. After an apprenticeship with the engraver James Basire, he studied at the Royal Academy Schools in 1779, but his stay there was short owing to his intense dislike of Joshua Reynolds. During this period of training, Blake became interested in the work of Raphael and Michelangelo, and he also studied the effigies on the medieval tombs in Westminster Abbey. In these formative years, his friends included John Flaxman and, at a later date, Henri Fuseli. He was widely read and, even as a boy, was writing poems of remarkable originality. By the time that he had reached his thirties, he had found scope for his genius in a series of illuminated books, the text, illustrations and printing all being the work of the artist himself. These included *Songs of Innocence*, 1789, *Songs of Experience*, 1794, and *The Book of Urizen*.

Blake produced this celebrated and powerful design of *Urizen creating the Universe*, known as *The Ancient of Days* (Daniel, Chapter VII, 22), around 1794, and used it as a coloured-print Frontispiece to his *Europe, A Prophecy*. The motif of the compasses is the symbol for the act of creation as described in Proverbs, Chapter VIII, 27: "When he prepared the heavens, I was there: when he set a compass upon the face of the depth". This symbolic representation of the act also corresponds with Milton's description in *Paradise Lost*, Book VII, 224-231:

> Then staid the fervid Wheeles, and in his hand
> He took the golden Compasses, prepar'd
> In God's Eternal store, to circumscribe
> This Universe, and all created things:
> One foot he center'd, and the other turn'd
> Round through the vast profunditie obscure,

> And said, thus farr extend, thus farr thy bounds,
> This be thy just Circumference, O World.

Blake refers in his own writings to the symbol of the compasses. In the Preludium of *Europe* are the words: "And who shall bind the infinite with an eternal band? To compass it with swaddling bands?" Then, in *The First Book of Urizen*, also 1794, Urizen "formed golden compasses, and began to explore the Abyss". On page 96 of the artist's *Notebook* in the British Museum, there is a rough sketch for the design of a figure holding compasses as in this design, with the inscription "who shall bind the Infinite".

In his *Prophetic Books* of 1793-5, Blake invented his own mythology to illustrate his beliefs and express his ideas on the Creation. Urizen, the Creator, is a character to be identified with the Old Testament's Jehova, an evil oppressor who decreed law, thus stifling Imagination. The conflicts caused by this act of repression are recounted in the books. Urizen appears as a venerable figure, bearded and with long, flowing hair, the traditional image for God the Father as envisaged by Michelangelo among other artists. Blake used this image not only in *Urizen*, but also in some of the large colour prints of 1795—*Elohim creating Adam* and *God judging Adam*, both in the Tate Gallery— and in the biblical watercolours drawn for Thomas Butts.

The artist completed several versions of the *Ancient of Days* in different colourations. It is a striking example of the powerful imagination which dominated Blake's style, with its bold design and dramatic movement. This version has been identified with the impression coloured by Blake "when bolstered-up in his bed only a few days before he died", according to J.T. Smith in *Nollekens and his Times*, 1829.

FWH

Manfred and the Witch of the Alps 1837

John Martin (1789-1853) British

Watercolour, bodycolour and gum 388 x 558 mm

Purchased in 1974 with the aid of grants from the Victoria and Albert Museum
Purchase Grant Fund and the Friends of the Whitworth (D.6.1974)

This spectacular watercolour was first exhibited with a companion scene, *Manfred on the Jungfrau,* at the Society of British Artists in 1838. Both drawings illustrate scenes from Byron's poetic drama *Manfred,* first published in 1817. The poems of Byron provided artists with ready dramatic subjects to which they were quick to respond and such was the popularity of his work that few people who saw this drawing at its first exhibition would have been unfamiliar with its subject.

The poem tells, in dramatic form, the story of Manfred who, as a punishment for dabbling in the black arts, is pursued by a band of Furies. He climbs the Jungfrau mountain and is about to throw himself off when he is halted by a passing hunter; it is this moment that the companion scene, now in Birmingham City Art Gallery, illustrates. In Act II, Scene ii Manfred descends to a lower valley to seek help from the spirit world. The Whitworth drawing illustrates the moment when using his dark skills, Manfred summons up the Witch of the Alps: "Manfred takes some of the water into the palm of his hand, and flings it in the air, muttering the abjuration. After a pause, the Witch of the Alps rises beneath the arch of the sun bow of the torrent."

He then tells her his story: how he had shunned the company of men in pursuit of knowledge and "sciences untaught, save in the old time"; how he had loved a girl but "destroyed her" because his evil dealings had caused her pure heart to "wither"; and how, because of this, he is constantly attended by furies who will permit him no rest. The Witch replies with an offer: "but if thou Wilt swear obedience to my will, and do My bidding, it may help thee to thy wishes."

Manfred refuses, saying why should he be slave to "the spirits whose presence I command". The remainder of the poem tells of his further refusals to give up his powers, and his death following the apparition of his beloved who cannot promise him that they will ever meet again.

Aside from the literary subject, which actually takes up a small part of the scene and is for the most part supplied by the viewer, the artist's main concern is to create an overwhelming image of the sublime power of the mountains. Martin never visited Switzerland and clearly the two views make no attempt to be topographically correct; instead the artist manipulates every aspect of perspective, scale and colour to produce a scene of almost hallucinatory power. It is indicative of Martin's skill as a watercolourist that on a comparatively small sheet of paper he can create as dazzling an image of the immensity of nature as in his much larger canvases. He does so by stretching the medium to the limit: mixing watercolour and gouache (an opaque medium closer in effect to oil painting) as well as using gum in some of the darker areas to give extra depth and richness. Martin also scrapes out areas to create the misty effect around the Witch and uses various drying techniques to create different textural effects. The strange shadow next to Manfred shows a change of position of the main figure and what shows through is the initial stopping out of an area reserved for the figure.

Descriptions of Martin's work frequently have recourse to images taken from the convulsions of nature. There are no direct references in this work to the sort of destructive power seen in some of his biblical illustrations; nonetheless, the form of the mountains reflect then current theories about the cataclysmic origins of landforms. The great sheer rock faces, the narrow gorge formed by some unimaginable torrent and the wave-like rock strata, seemingly the product of enormous heat and pressure, are all evidence of a violent past and a genesis which saw the unleashing of the fullest and most ungovernable forces of nature. This certainly was the theory of the geologist Leopold Cuvier who had approved of Martin's interpretation of the theme of *The Deluge* of 1834 and was the most important exponent of the Catastrophic Theory of land formation. Given this approach the destiny of Byron's protagonist in the human drama of damnation pales into insignificance.   GS

The Lake of Lucerne, Moonlight, the Rigi in the Distance c1841

Joseph Mallord William Turner (1775-1851) British

Watercolour and bodycolour with scratching out 230 x 307mm

Purchased in 1891 with a fund presented by the Guarantors of the Manchester Royal Jubilee Exhibition, 1887 (D.16.1887)

When Turner visited Lake Lucerne in Switzerland in 1841 he made a number of sketches, many of them featuring Mount Rigi, with the intention of developing selected subjects into finished watercolours. The artist already knew Switzerland well by then, having made his first tour of the country in 1802, which took him to Geneva, Chamonix, Thun, Lucerne and St Gotthard, and he returned for a second tour in 1836. After his 1802 journey, the artist produced some of his grandest and most ambitious landscapes in watercolour and it was these works which attracted the notice of one of his most generous patrons, Walter Fawkes of Farnley Hall in Yorkshire. After the 1841 tour, Turner worked up some of his sketches and by the spring of 1842 he had as many as fifteen watercolour studies to offer his dealer, Thomas Griffith of Norwood, as samples from which he was prepared to make a set of ten larger watercolours. In fact, he had already completed four subjects in order that clients could see how the finished versions looked including *The Splugen Pass, The Blue Rigi*, and the *Bay of Uri*. Griffith was troubled by these four works, pointing out to the artist that they were "a little different from your usual style". All the same, he invited four of Turner's most enthusiastic patrons to view them—H.A.J. Munro of Novar, Godfrey Windus, Elhanan Bicknell and the Ruskins, father and son. Griffith managed to sell these watercolours and obtained commissions for five other subjects, but the tenth remained in his own hands. The additional watercolours included *Brunnen, Lucerne from the Walls, Coblenz* and *Constance*. Munro of Novar acquired five of the watercolours from this unique set which, as Ruskin later remarked, were unlike any drawings that Turner had ever made previously, and he "never made any like them again". They can undoubtedly be regarded as the artist's crowning achievement in watercolour.

Although the Whitworth's *Lake of Lucerne* does not belong to that group, it is thought that it might be an unused sample study of 1841, as it is close in treatment and finish to the preparatory studies for the *Rigi* subjects. However, Turner adopted the same practice of providing samples after his subsequent visits to Switzerland in 1842 and 1843, so there is some slight doubt over the precise year in which he completed this watercolour.

The region around Lucerne became one of the artist's favourite haunts on his last visits to the Continent, for he was in the same area in 1842, 1843 and 1844, and many of his most brilliant watercolours of that period are of the magnificent country surrounding the Rigi range, between Lakes Lucerne and Zug. Inspired by such spectacular scenery, the sixty-seven year old artist produced a large number of sketches which resulted in a series of intensely atmospheric and emotionally charged watercolours—"every day, on these excursions, furnished him with many more subjects for complete pictures than he could at all sufficiently express" *(Notes by Mr Ruskin, 1878)*. In many of these late watercolours the sublime and majestic forms of the mountains float effortlessly above tranquil waters, sometimes surrounded by early morning mists, at other times bathed in moonlight, as here, or in a sunset glow.

FWH

Springtime 1853

James Thomas Linnell (1826-1905) British

Oil on canvas 714 x 962mm

Presented by Miss Heaven in 1896 (0.1.1896)

The file on one of the most popular images in the Gallery is surprisingly one of the slimmest, but if ever a work appeared to stand on its own without need of explanation, it would be *Springtime*. The image of children picking wild flowers on a bright Spring day with the trees ready to burst into leaf and a crop emerging from a ploughed field is a universal, timeless evocation of season in complete contrast to the allegorical treatment of Summer in *Flora* produced a few years later by William Morris and Edward Burne-Jones (p.86). There is nothing to disturb the gloriously idyllic depiction of country life; even the old man walking in the distance, supported by a friend, only adds a gently elegiac quality in contrast.

The reasons for the painting's popularity are not difficult to explain. Quite clearly both the subject and the very precise, almost photographic detail are immediately accessible. But here lies one of the dangers of the work, for we may be tempted, quite unfairly, to use its attention to detail as a standard by which to judge works, such as the Howard Hodgkin (p.130) which are trying to do other things. Linnell has used tiny touches of pigment over a white ground in order to enhance the purity of the colour in the manner of the Pre-Raphaelites. But in painting, or appearing to paint, every leaf, he may be thought to have sacrificed other qualities. Another danger is that this work exerts an emotional pull on the viewer which, although it may stop short of the sentimental, is nonetheless very powerful; it is certainly more to do with what the viewer brings to the painting, in the form of memories and associations, than with any intrinsic merit in the work itself. The artist puts into the painting all the right ingredients and it is we who complete the picture; in literary terms this has been called 'The Stock Response'. To account for our pleasure in the work we are likely to praise the artist for his brilliance, but, in part at least, we are responding to things outside the picture. This is not to say that the painting is good or bad, but that pleasure is not related to quality in a simple relationship.

We know very little about the artist, simply that he was the second son of the artist John Linnell and that he exhibited at the Royal Academy from 1850. Linnell painted mainly in the South East of England and in particular in Surrey around his home in Reigate. Part of the attraction of the work is the familiar nature of the landscape; everybody feels they know its location. But it is quite possible that no precise location ever existed; behind all of its truthful detail it may be a fabrication. The work thus embodies an idea, an idealised vision of the English landscape, and it is this which makes it so attractive; a more precise topographical title and content would destroy the universal nature of the scene.

There are those, however, who think that the scene is just too good to be true, that if you dig a little deeper you might discover that the agricultural situation in Surrey in 1853 was such that children you did see in the woods (rather than working as sweated labour on the farm) would in truth be wearing ragged and torn clothes. It may well be that the greatest danger of a magnificently truthful painting, in the sense of visual veracity, is that it can hide dreadful lies; that for an urban middle-class audience it can dress a consoling myth about the countryside in a garment that seems as natural as nature herself.   GS

Flounce or collar of Brussels Point de Gaze Lace

Belgium: c1860-70

Linen thread 203 x 1118 mm (outer edge)

Presented by Mrs Lionel Pilkington in 1954 (T.10076)

Brussels *point de gaze* was one of the finest and most costly hand-made laces produced in the nineteenth century. It was shown as a new development of the Brussels lacemakers at the Great Exhibition of 1851 at Crystal Palace, and enjoyed immediate success. *Point de gaze* is identifiable by the delicate, gauzy net ground to which it owes its name, and by the emphasis on naturalistic floral motifs in its design. Naturalistic effects were sought right across popular mid-Victorian textile design, and these were heightened in Brussels lace by the alternation of dense and open buttonholing stitch in the leaves and floral motifs, which gives the appearance of shading. Later, in the 1860s and 1870s, *point de gaze* began to show relief effects, as flowers were given several layers of petals only partially attached to the ground. It is the contrast between this three-dimensional realism and the gossamer-light ground which distinguishes *point de gaze* from other contemporary needlepoint laces, such as the French Alençon.

Brussels was best known for its bobbin laces but, during the course of the nineteenth century, it became one of the most important centres in Europe for the manufacture of needlelace. *Point de gaze* was developed as a direct competitor to Alençon which, in 1850, was the most expensive and prestigious of the hand-made laces. There are differences: unlike Alençon the motifs in *point de gaze* are not accentuated by a raised *cordonnet* or outline, and the net ground is lighter and more fragile. Because it could be made rather more quickly, *point de gaze* was also less expensive than Alençon, a factor which contributed to its success.

The mid-nineteenth century saw the beginning of a boom in the lace industry. Lace is a fabric dependent for its success or failure on the vagaries of fashion, and from 1850 to 1870 lace played a prominent part in all evening and most day wear. Skirts might have a deep lace flounce at the hem, or a number of narrower flounces arranged in zig-zag formation or other decorative manner. Lace shawls and fans were an important accessory, whilst handkerchiefs, veils, underwear, and night clothes might all be either made of, or trimmed with, lace.

Throughout its history lace has been used, particularly in dress, to denote wealth and status. By the 1850s, however, improvements in lace machinery meant that good imitations of some hand-made laces could be produced at a price which almost everyone could afford. The makers of high quality laces, like Alençon and *point de gaze*, therefore, competed by offering to the very wealthy a finer product than the machines could produce. Indeed, the period from 1850 to 1870 saw the growth of a luxury lace trade which approached the eighteenth century in conspicuous consumption of its products.

The demand was much reduced in the closing quarter of the century, as fashions changed and the manufacture of machine lace continued to increase and improve. Brussels *point de gaze* was made until the end of the nineteenth century, but on a much reduced scale after 1870. JH

O-hashi Atake no yudachi 1857

(Sudden shower over O-hashi Bridge at Atake)
Plate from Meisho Edo Hyakkei (The Hundred Famous Views of Edo)
Designed by Ando Hiroshige (1797-1858) Japanese

Published by Uoya Eikichi (Uoei) of Shitaya
Woodcut, printed in colours; image size 338 x 220 mm
Presented by the executors of Joseph Knight in 1953 (5638)

The 'Edo', in the title of the series of colour woodblock prints from which this image is taken, is the name by which the modern city of Tokyo was formerly known; it is also the name given to the period of Japanese history, from 1600-1868, during which the effective government of the country was based at the centre of the city of Edo. This was headed by a succession of warriors, or shoguns, of the Tokugawa family, whilst the Imperial court was some distance away in Kyoto, the Emperor himself stripped of all but ceremonial functions. It was during the 'Edo' period that the kind of printmaking of which Hiroshige's landscape is an example, became fashionable and popular; such prints became known as *ukiyo-e*—pictures of the floating world. The word was originally a Buddhist term, used to refer to an undesirable state of affairs—the illusory qualities of this world of ceaselesss reincarnation. Gradually, however, the word acquired more approbatory overtones, suggesting more positive feelings about human life, its pleasures, amusements and fashions. In seventeenth-century Edo it came to be applied to the distinct style of painting, and to the book illustrations and prints derived from it, which grew up to record the pleasures and entertainments of the urban culture that had developed as the new capital had grown and prospered.

Both literary and visual tastes were important aspects of this developing culture. *Ukiyo-e* prints had their origins as illustrations to the popular novels and volumes of poetry, as well as guides to brothels and sex manuals produced to satisfy the market. Members of the aristocracy clearly regarded it as beneath their dignity to patronise the work of painters of the *ukiyo-e* school, but such paintings were nonetheless sufficiently high in price for only the wealthiest of men of a lower social status to afford. It was therefore the colour woodblock images, printed on paper and distributed in huge numbers, which enabled a vastly extended range of the population to share and enjoy the new imagery.

It is, however, misleading to think of a print such as this as the work of one man, Ando Hiroshige; it was in fact a truly co-operative effort between a publisher, an artist, a team of engravers and a team of printers. The publisher was usually the main instigator of the project, providing organisation and financial backing. The artist would make a line drawing on very thin paper of the image to be produced, handing it over to a team of engravers, who would paste the drawing face down onto a wooden block (usually cherry or pear wood), cut along the grain. The most skilled engraver would then cut around the lines of the drawing (destroying it in the process) and leave ridges of wood standing in relief. This line block would be passed to a printer, who would take a few proofs, returning one to the artist for him to indicate the areas to be printed in colour. The engravers would then cut further blocks, sometimes up to ten or more, one for each colour; these were passed to the printers to print, building up the image colour by colour. The printing was often done without a press; pigment made from vegetable colours, mixed with size from rice, would be brushed onto the blocks, and the image transferred by placing a sheet of paper over the block and rubbing it on the back with a tool known as a baren; this was a circular pad made from a coil of twisted bamboo sheath cord with a covering made from the outer skin of the bamboo plant.

The particular qualities that we admire in this print are not therefore only due to Hiroshige's skill in observing and recording atmospheric effects and weather conditions, they also derive from the skill of the woodcutters and printers. The latter translated the artist's observations, partly by outlining the foreground figures and the bridge in black but leaving the background trees undefined so they we are given the impression of seeing them imperfectly through a haze of rain; and partly by varying the inking of the blocks so that sky and water are suggested by graded tones of a single colour. The sky is further enhanced by the actual grain of the wooden block which gives texture to the area, whilst the tones of the mist-obscured foliage beneath the sky are suggested by shifting blends of grey.   SH

Fruit

Designed by William Morris (1834-1896) British, c1862

Manufactured by Jeffrey & Co, 1864

Portion of hand-printed wallpaper, colour print from wood blocks 673 x 548 mm

Presented by The Wall Paper Manufacturers Ltd in 1967 (W.89.1967)

The business relationship of William Morris and Metford Warner spanned more than a quarter of a century and resulted in the production of more than fifty wallpapers, of which all but a dozen or so were designed by Morris himself.

When his first patterns, designed in 1862, were produced, the firm of which he was partner and business manager had been in existence for three years, successfully producing stained glass, painted woodwork and church furnishings. The wallpapers were not issued until 1864 and it may have been Morris's unsuccessful efforts to print the first, *Trellis*, by himself, by means of etched zinc plates and oil colours instead of the usual distemper, which led to the delay. Ultimately the designs were transferred to pear wood blocks and handed over to Jeffrey & Co, a wallpaper manufacturing firm whose reputation had been considerably enhanced by its exhibits at both the Great Exhibition of 1851 and the International Exhibition of 1862.

Morris's first three designs, with their simple, naturalistic motifs, were not immediately popular. Indeed, he was advised that "considering the limited sales" of the papers it was not worth issuing more new designs. Thus, it was not until 1872 that he resumed this branch of his activities, by which time Metford Warner had become Managing Director of Jeffrey & Co.

Warner has been credited "more than any other man" with responsibility for the prominence of the English wallpaper industry at the end of the nineteenth century. His reputation was achieved by the high technical quality of the products, together with his practice of employing architects and designers who had not designed wallpapers before. However, it is ironic that Morris, who prided himself on his ability to master new techniques, was forced to hand over the production of his papers to another firm and he found it impossible to resist becoming practically involved in the production process, albeit in a supervisory capacity. He checked the cutter's tracings before the designs were transferred to the blocks and, once the printing was under way, he was "always at the front, directing and encouraging and forcibly demonstrating as to the incorrigible stupidity of those who did not grasp his ideas". He was particularly concerned that his directions should be followed rigorously; "Tell them not to improve my colourings", was the message that the long-suffering Warner had to convey to the factory from "the master in blue blouse, bare feet in slippers and hands blue from the dye vat".

Although Morris' later patterns show a move towards a more formal approach, the early designs exhibited a naively romantic character. This is most evident in the "unashamedly three-dimensional" motifs of *Fruit*, and contrasted strongly with the more austere, geometric styles which, by 1855, were being produced in quantity by all the leading manufacturers, including Jeffrey & Co. Thus, the impact of *Fruit* is likely to have been at the conservative, bourgeois end of the market rather than with the *avant-garde*. However, had it not been for Morris' insistence that only the labour intensive traditional hand-printing methods be applied to the production of his papers, many of the designs would perhaps have been available to a wider public. Instead, during the 1870s, they cost between 2/6d and 16/- per roll, and were beyond the resources of all but the middle and upper layers of society. It is paradoxical that Morris' own concern with the retention of the richness and subtlety of his colours in the production of high-quality decorations put them out of reach of the masses with whom he wished to share his "keen delight" in the artistic representation of the English countryside. Morris' designs were printed by Jeffrey & Co until the 1920s, when Metford Warner retired after fifty-eight years as Partner and Manager. Soon afterwards the firm was taken over and although *Fruit* is still produced by traditional hand-printing with pear wood blocks, the continuing popularity of the Morris designs has been ensured by modern methods of mass production, and by changes in colouring which render them harmonious with late twentieth-century interiors. CW

Romeo and Juliet 1867

Ford Madox Brown (1821-1893) British

Watercolour and bodycolour on paper 480 x 330 mm

Purchased in 1917 (D.20.1917)

This highly finished watercolour of the balcony scene from Shakespeare's *Romeo and Juliet* of 1867 illustrates the anguished parting of the two lovers as dawn arrives:

> *... Look, love, what envious streaks*
> *Do lace the severing clouds in yonder East.*
> *Night's candles are burnt out, and jocund day*
> *Stands tiptoe on the misty mountain tops.*
> *I must be gone and live, or stay and die.*

Madox Brown was clearly not interested in illustrating the play in production. The figures are not depicted as actors, whilst the viewer is not part of an audience but a privileged eavesdropper on a private moment. The artist's interest in rendering historical details such as costume, architecture and the view out over medieval Verona, all go beyond the efforts of any scene painter in the recreation of a setting.

This attention to detail is matched by a parallel commitment to emotional or psychological truth. The term 'bowdlerize', to censor on the grounds of morality, was a nineteenth-century one, originating in an attempt to make Shakespeare conform to contemporary standards of morality. There were many who wished to play down the passionate physical nature of the love between Romeo and Juliet, whom Shakespeare informs us is twelve years old. The gestures of both protagonists, totally absorbed in each other, underline the artist's intention, expressed in a letter to his patron, that this image, quite aside from the literal rendering of a story, was to be seen as a universal image of overwhelming passion.

Shakespearean subjects remained popular with artists throughout the eighteenth and nineteenth centuries; 1400 works were shown at the Royal Academy alone in the period 1769-1900. There had been a marked preference for grand historical set pieces, many with famous actors in character. The new century saw a shift to more intimate domestic scenes, concentrating in particular on the heroines; a single character often stood for the whole play.

This work was not produced for public exhibition, however, but was commissioned by a Manchester collector, Frederick Craven, who was one of Brown's most loyal patrons. Rossetti characterised him, rather unfairly, as a "good paymaster... a grave and (let us say in a whisper) rather stupid enthusiast of the inarticulate business type, with a mystic reverence for the English watercolour school". It is worth looking at the circumstances of the commission and at the other versions which Brown produced because they tell us much about the economics of art production in the period.

The first point to make is that the labour involved in developing and researching a new subject made it essential for Brown to sell at least one replica. Usually the initial commission was for an oil which often required the preparation of a half-size cartoon as well as a number of working drawings. Watercolour replicas could then be produced with little extra effort according to demand. In this case, since Craven only collected watercolours, the oil version, which was started at the same time, remained unfinished until 1869 when a buyer was found. Brown also produced a watercolour duplicate (1868-71), and in 1876 he even worked up the original cartoon for sale. From the artist's notes we know that the Whitworth watercolour was begun on June 1st and finished on September 16th and cost £131 5s. The oil was begun immediately after and took another two and a half working months to complete; it was sold for £325.

Like many nineteenth-century artists Brown used a mixed watercolour/bodycolour technique which in its richness of colour and complex structure was more akin to an oil painting than the gentler tinted drawings of the eighteenth century. In part this reflected a gradual change in the function of watercolours from objects to be viewed in a portfolio in a library to paintings hung on a wall. The gold mount and frame are an integral part of the work and would have helped to harmonise the rich, saturated colours of Brown's palette with Craven's home. GS

La Donna della Finestra 1870
(The Woman at the Window)
Dante Gabriel Rossetti (1828-1882) British

Pastel on coloured paper 848 x 720 mm

Purchased in 1921 (D.35.1921)

La Donna della Finestra (The Woman at the Window) was one of a series of drawings made by Rossetti in the years 1868-70 with Jane Morris as the model. The group was produced in pastels on tinted paper of a uniform size; this drawing, like a number of others, is on two pieces of paper and the join can still be seen. This much only is simple.

To begin with, the title of the drawing is misleading. Though it is clearly the starting point for another more finished pastel, also dated 1870 and titled *La Donna della Finestra,* this is primarily a portrait drawing. The sitter is actually shown resting her hands on a table and it is not impossible that the title is a retrospective one. Did Rossetti pose her in this way with the subject already in mind, or did a comfortable and convenient pose for a private portrait drawing suggest the subject of the subsequent variations on the Whitworth drawing? Rossetti frequently adapted portrait studies by adding an attribute or inscription to produce a more saleable, more public work. In the case of the finished pastel, now in Bradford, the inscription from Dante's *Vita Nuova* on the window sill transforms the pose of the Whitworth portrait into a subject full of interesting implications.

Leaving aside the view that a shift from a private portrait to a historical subject made economic sense, the changes which occurred between the two works are also evidence of Rossetti's extraordinary capacity for self dramatisation. The *Donna della Finestra* in Dante's poem is the woman who, on looking down from her window, takes pity on the poet grieving for the loss of his beloved Beatrice. The full context for the quotation used on the Bradford drawing is as follows:

> *No woman's countenance has ever worn*
> *In such miraculous degree the hue*
> *Of love and pity's look,...*
> *My wasted eyes I find I cannot keep*
> *From gazing at you ever and again,*
> *For by tearful longing they are led*

It is characteristic of Rossetti that his close personal association with his namesake, Dante, should be extended to Jane Morris who thus becomes his own 'Lady of Pity' (his alternative title for the work), consoling him for the loss of his beloved wife, Elizabeth Siddal.

Such a simplistic biographical reading of the work is, taken on its own, an unsatisfactory analysis of its meaning, however much Rossetti's obsessive self-mythologising encourages such interpretations. The Whitworth drawing also fulfilled a much more prosaic economic function. In 1879 Rossetti wrote to Jane Morris that he had had "the rare luck to sell the picture of you—*La Donna della Finestra.* Ellis has bought it. Last year... he admired the cartoon, and when I told him I proposed painting it, he wished to see the picture!... So the old studies of you may go on being useful yet." It is likely that the Whitworth drawing is the one Rossetti refers to as the cartoon and that it had remained in his studio partly as a bait for the commission for a more remunerative oil painting.

The finished oil, produced nine years after the Whitworth drawing, develops the image further. It gives more specific details and plays further on the convention of the window frame being an equivalent to the picture frame. But the central point remains unaltered. How are we, the viewers, to react to the fierce obsessive stare of the sitter/subject? In spite of the title this image is hardly a consoling one. The stare of the woman is actually sanctioned by the historical subject, but mediated by our knowledge of the artist's relationship with his model it takes on new meanings. If we read the drawing as a literary subject the viewer must identify with Dante, but if we see it more as a portrait we perhaps inevitably feel implicated in the artist's fantasy of possession and deification which he spins around Jane Morris; it is this which is so disturbing. GS

Indoor Gossip, Cairo 1873

John Frederick Lewis (1805-1876) British

Oil on panel 304 x 202 mm

Purchased in 1961 with the aid of a grant from the Victoria and Albert Museum
Purchase Grant Fund (O.1.1961)

This work was exhibited with its pair, *Outdoor Gossip*, at the Royal Academy Summer Exhibition in 1873. Together the two scenes contrasted the enclosed, indoor life of women with the active, outdoor life of men in a society which reinforced to an even greater degree than Victorian Britain the exclusiveness of male and female spheres of influence.

Many writers have identified this scene as being located in a hareem. The narrow, rather flat space and the prominence of the mashrabiyya or screen lattice reinforce the sense of enclosure which to the Western imagination was closely associated with the hareem. The male fantasy of the hareem also centered around the idea of beautiful women idling away the day in sunny, colourful and heat-filled interiors; and this myth was reinforced by countless paintings exhibited at the French Salon and the Royal Academy of bathers, odalisques and denizens of the hareem in various states of undress and engaged in all manner of frivolous and languid activities. If we analyse the viewpoint in the picture we become uncomfortably aware of our intrusion, analogous to spying through a keyhole, into a private world which we as Westerners would have never have been able to enter.

Although the details of the interior and the costume all have a ring of authenticity and are clearly the product of careful study during Lewis' long stay in Egypt the composition has more features in common with Western traditions and in particular with Dutch seventeenth-century genre painting. The presence of the mirror and the indication of a space leading into the distance on the left, together with a careful attention to detail and the beautiful rendering of rich materials and textures recall the work of artists such as de Hoogh and Vermeer; as does the concentration on the fall of light from the lattice on to the wall. The work also reminds one of another tradition that was strong in Holland: that of the allegory of the senses. Here both the sense of touch and sight are carefully emphasised. Traditionally sight was represented by a mirror, which, as in this case, could also emphasise the theme of female vanity. It is to be assumed that the women are dressing, or playing at dressing, to please the men who are shown in the companion scene.

Lewis arrived in Cairo in 1841 and spent ten years there. He set up home in a traditional house and dressed in native costume and he was reported by a number of his compatriots to live the life of an opulent Oriental nobleman. Lewis also travelled widely in Egypt and everywhere sketched and studied. On his return to Britain he exhibited a number of his works to much acclaim and, although he was forced by economic circumstance to change from watercolour to oil painting in the late 1850s, he continued to paint views such as this until the end of his life. Lewis was not the first to travel to the Middle East in search of an exotic, colourful and unspoilt culture; he was a part of a generation of artists who ranged further afield than mainland Europe in search of new experiences. But although he was one of the most dedicated and sympathetic visitors Lewis was in no way able, or willing, to transcend all of the myths surrounding the East.

Since this work was painted twenty years after Lewis' return from Egypt one might argue that the real subject of such a view is not the actual look of the scenery and social habits of Cairo but that they are instead simply the pretext for a loving analysis of the play of light on fabric and walls rendered with a jewel-like touch. Lewis, unlike his audience who had no way of testing the reality of the dream-like images of the East which artists presented to them, must have been aware of the ways in which such scenes fell short of actuality. The fact that there was a ready market for such scenes and that so many artists worked in this genre suggests that the audience was not simply responding to the beauty of Lewis' handling of paint and that in some way they answered the need of his audience to believe in a fantasy image of the East as an exotic, colourful and, of course, decadent place.

GS

Flora c1885

Designed by Edward Burne-Jones (1833-1898)
and William Morris (1834-1896) British

Woven at Merton Abbey
Wool and silk tapestry on linen warps 3010 x 2095 mm
Purchased in 1888 (T.8353)

Flora, and her companion piece *Pomona,* were the first large-scale figure subjects to be carried out in woven tapestry at William Morris' Merton Abbey workshops. Personifications of Summer and Autumn respectively, they were woven between 1884 and 1885 by William Knight, William Sleath and John Martin, using figure drawings made by Burne-Jones a year or so earlier. All of the decorative details of the tapestries, including the acanthus leaf grounds, were supplied by Morris himself, whereas in later tapestries such work was invariably left to his assistant, John Henry Dearle. The inscriptions on the scrolls at the top and bottom of the tapestries are from verses, also by Morris, and were later published in his *Poems by the Way* (1891). Both tapestries were shown at the Royal Jubilee Exhibition in Manchester in 1887 and were purchased for display at the opening of Grove House in 1890.

The use of tapestry in a domestic setting was unusual by the mid-nineteenth century, but antiquarian research had emphasised its importance in medieval decoration. When Morris began weaving tapestry in 1878, initially on a small loom set up in his bedroom, what he had in mind was no less than a full-scale revival of the craft on medieval lines. All Morris & Co tapestries, including *Flora,* were inspired by late medieval tapestries, especially Flemish examples of the late fifteenth and early sixteenth centuries. Morris particularly admired the shallow planes and ornamental qualities of medieval tapestry, which had disappeared during the post-Renaissance period as tapestry began to imitate the effects of oil painting, and this explains the clarity and richness of detail and colour of *Flora.* The acanthus leaf grounds derive from the patterning on so-called 'large leaf verdure' tapestries manufactured in France and Flanders in the sixteenth century, and the clumps of flowering plants in the foreground evoke the *millefleurs* grounds which were also a characteristic of medieval Flemish work.

After the move to Merton Abbey in 1881, Morris & Co tapestries were worked on the high warp upright loom used in medieval tapestry production. In this technique, the warp threads are arranged vertically and the weaver works from the back, being able to check the progress of the work by looking through the warp threads at a mirror hanging in front. Burne-Jones' original figure drawings were usually quite small, some 380-500 mm high on average, and were enlarged photographically to scale to provide the working cartoons for the weavers. The artist would then work over the photographs, highlighting those parts of the drawing which particularly required it, usually the hands and faces.

In a lecture on 'Textiles' given to the Arts and Crafts Exhibition Society in 1888, Morris spoke of tapestry as "the noblest of the weaving arts... in which there is nothing mechanical." He expressed great disdain for the contemporary practice of reproducing Old Master paintings at the Gobelins workshops in France which, for him, had "changed tapestry-weaving from a fine art into a mere upholsterer's toy". His ideal at Merton Abbey was to give back to his weavers the artistic freedom to improvise on a cartoon, particularly in the choice of colour, which the medieval craftsman had possessed.

Tapestry weaving is a slow and costly business and Morris' clients were charged from twelve to sixteen guineas per square foot, depending on the complexity of the design and the status of the weavers employed. His incursion into tapestry weaving threw into sharp relief the dichotomy between Morris' cherished belief that art should not be the exclusive preserve of a privileged few and the fact that he spent much of his career, as he put it, "ministering to the swinish luxury of the rich".

Flora proved a popular design. At least eleven smaller versions exist, woven under Dearle from 1895 onwards. They lack Morris' verse quatrains and have different grounds.   JH

I am the handmaid of the earth · I broider fair her glorious gown
and deck her on her days of mirth · with many garland of renown

and while earths little ones are fain · and play about the mothers hem
I scatter every gift I gain · from sun and wind to gladden them

The Parlement of Foules: the Proem 1896

Plate from The Works of Geoffrey Chaucer now newly imprinted
Illustration designed by Edward Burne-Jones (1833-1898) British

Borders and initial letters designed by Edward Burne-Jones and William Morris
Blocks cut by W.H. Hooper; printed by William Morris at the Kelmscott Press, Hammersmith
Wood engraving; page size 423 x 290 mm
Presented by A.E. Anderson in 1934 (5236)

The main events narrated in Geoffrey Chaucer's *The Parlement of Foules,* take place in the context of a dream. The poet-figure who introduces himself at the beginning of the poem tells us that he has recently been reading the *Somnium Scipionis* (The Dream of Scipio) in which the Roman proconsul Scipio appears to his son in a dream, and takes him up to the heavens where he shows him the mysteries of the future life. When nightfall prevents Chaucer's poet from reading any more, he too falls asleep, and dreams that Scipio comes to his bedside. The Roman takes him to a hillside where the birds are assembled before the goddess Nature on St Valentine's day to choose their mates. A dispute breaks out as to which shall choose the most magnificent of the birds, the eagle, and, after discussion amongst the 'parlement', the goddess rules that the eagle herself shall select her own partner.

The Works of Geoffrey Chaucer was the most important production of the Kelmscott Press, a printing and publishing house founded by William Morris in 1891. The book was unusual for the Press, since few Kelmscott editions contained any illustrations; many were entirely typographical, whilst others were embellished only with initial letters and borders. Initially Morris planned to have sixty illustrations in the Chaucer, but this was gradually increased to eighty-seven, as Burne-Jones, the designer of the illustrations, became increasingly obsessed with the project. It is however not simply the illustrations that are responsible for the impact of pages like the one illustrated opposite. The impressiveness of the book as a whole depends as much on Morris' decorative borders and elaborate initial letters as on the illustrations. Burne-Jones himself was aware of the fact that his style of drawing was not always robust enough to complement the vigour of some of Chaucer's tales, and he admitted that he had not wanted to illustrate certain of the *Canterbury Tales,* clearly referring to the more 'bawdy' ones such as *The Miller's Tale.* Morris had evidently urged him to try, but Burne-Jones felt that he "ever had more robust and daring parts than I could assume".

The Kelmscott Press was founded by Morris in the last years of his life (he died in 1896), when illness had already taken its toll. It was founded in quite a different spirit to that in which the 'Firm', Morris, Marshall, Faulkner and Co, had been launched thirty years earlier. Then, Morris had been determined to reform the 'shoddy' quality of the decorative arts produced for what he considered to be a philistine age. He laid emphasis instead on sound workmanship in good materials, and on richness of decorative detail. He was to find that this second objective could only be achieved through finding purchasers for his work amongst the wealthiest class and, this, combined with his concern for the working lives and conditions of the people making the objects compelled him towards a practical commitment to socialism. Right to the end of his life he maintained that "I have not changed my mind on Socialism", but by the time the Kelmscott Press was founded he had little thought of reforming the world through his art. He saw the venture more as a personal experiment in the production of really beautiful books.

At first Morris intended neither to publish nor to sell the books, only to tackle the problems involved in designing typefaces, and making good quality paper and printing inks as a kind of private hobby. Eventually he was forced to try and offset the cost of such experiments by producing and selling limited editions of each work; the Chaucer, for example, was produced in an edition of 425 copies on paper and thirteen 'luxury' copies on vellum. The paper copies sold for £16 3s each, a price which was prohibitive for the general public, though necessary to meet the costs of the fine materials used and the reasonable wages which Morris insisted on paying the workers at Kelmscott. However Morris clearly felt that the energy he had devoted to the socialist cause during his younger life to some extent absolved him from the necessity of justifying the pleasures in which he indulged himself in later years; the Kelmscott Press was to him a source of relaxation and pleasure, and one in which his abilities both as a writer and a designer could be well used. SH

THE PARLEMENT OF FOULES. THE PROEM.

THE LYF SO SHORT, THE CRAFT SO LONG
to lerne,
Thassay so hard, so sharp the conquering,
The dredful joy, that alwey slit so yerne,
Al this mene I by love, that my feling
Astonyeth with his wonderful worching
So sore ywis, that whan I on him thinke,
Nat wot I wel wher that I wake or winke.

For al be that I knowe not love in dede,
Ne wot how that he quyteth folk hir hyre,
Yet happeth me ful ofte in bokes rede
Of his miracles, and his cruel yre;
Ther rede I wel he wol be lord and syre,
I dar not seyn, his strokes been so sore,
But God save swich a lord! I can no more.

Of usage, what for luste what for lore,
On bokes rede I ofte, as I yow tolde.
But wherfor that I speke al this? not yore
Agon, hit happed me for to beholde
Upon a boke, was write with lettres olde;
And therupon, a certeyn thing to lerne,
The longe day ful faste I radde and yerne.

For out of olde feldes, as men seith,
Cometh al this newe corn fro yeer to yere;
And out of olde bokes, in good feith,
Cometh al this newe science that men lere.
But now to purpos as of this matere...
To rede forth hit gan me so delyte,
That al the day me thoughte but a lyte.

This book of which I make mencioun,
Entitled was al thus, as I shal telle,
Tullius of the dreme of Scipioun;

Floor Rug

Iran (Qashqā'i): 1890-1895

Hand-knotted wool 2060 x 1490 mm
Purchased in 1974 with the aid of the
Friends of the Whitworth (T.85.1975)

The Whitworth began its collection of tribal rugs and other weavings in the early 1970s, when it began to seem likely that pastoral nomadism in Central Asia, and its associated crafts, was entering a period of perhaps terminal decline. It was decided to develop in Manchester a centre for the study of these crafts, and to purchase appropriate material—rugs, horse covers, saddle and storage bags, camel and horse trappings, costume and jewellery—whilst it was still readily available. The collection concentrates on the Qashqā'i of Iran, whose rugs are counted amongst the best of all Persian tribal weavings for their variety of design, clarity of colour and fineness of weave.

This Qashqā'i pile rug displays all the characteristics of a tribal piece, as well as possessing many features which identify it as typical of the Qashqā'i. In common with most tribal and village rugs the general lay-out is rectilinear, because, unlike a curvilinear design, it does not require a draughtsman to draw out the pattern to scale, whilst the comparatively loose knotting of tribal rugs is also ill-suited to curvilinear designs. Tribal rugs display great inventiveness in their design, for the women who weave them are free to improvise as they work, whilst their own family and tribal background will further influence the choice of motifs.

Emigration of tribes for political or military reasons, settlement and intermarriage have all, over the centuries, contributed to a diffusion of different tribal traditions, making it difficult sometimes to distinguish and classify the various types of rug from just one area. The Qashqā'i is a confederation of various tribes from Fars province in South-West Iran usually thought of as nomadic, though, in fact, considerable numbers have now become settled. Centuries ago, they were originally established in northern Iran and are, thus, related to the peoples of the Caucasus. This is evident from their rugs.

The highly geometricized diamond-shaped medallions and general lay-out of this rug, which is a typical Qashqā'i piece, owe much to the Caucasian influence, whilst their hooked outlines also betray Turkic origin. Another favourite Caucasian motif is the hexagon or octagon, which is here enclosed within the medallions and itself encloses either an eight-pointed star, the Chinese endless knot or an eight-lobed rosette. The formalised floral ornament in the main field and in the borders is borrowed from Persian workshop carpets, whilst other motifs, such as the *boteh*, are more universal. This motif, which appears as minor infilling ornament on this rug, is an enigmatic pattern of ancient Persian origin which is variously likened to the pine, the palm, a pear, or an almond. Another distinguishing feature of Qashqā'i rugs are the small animals spaced around the central medallions or used as infill. Here, a row of crested birds is alternately confronted and addorsed on either side of the medallions.

Qashqā'i rugs are renowned for the quality and purity of their colours, as well as the great variety of tones. The colours derive from tribal recipes, using common Iranian dyeplants, although the temptation to buy chemically-dyed wool, in the bazaar, is very strong, especially when certain colours are desired. This can result in wool dyed with both chemical and natural dyes being used in one rug. The wool itself is a highly valued commodity, being hard, long-stapled and glossy, and makes rugs from Fars quite easy to recognise.

Traditionally amongst the Qashqā'i, all the spinning, dyeing, weaving, and knotting are carried out by the women, who have thus played a crucial part in preserving cultural traditions. Genuine tribal rugs are woven on a horizontal or ground loom of ancient origin, which has the virtue of being easily unpegged, rolled up and packed during the tribe's migratory period. There is also, however, a flourishing village industry made up of settled tribespeople, of which this rug is an example. It bears all the hallmarks of a tribal design, but was produced commercially, whereas genuine tribal rugs were woven exclusively for use in the tent.   JH

Love and Death c1877-87

George Frederick Watts (1817-1904) British

Oil on canvas 2489 x 1168 mm

Presented by the artist in 1887 (0.1.1887)

Love and Death was the first work to enter the Whitworth's collection, its accession predating the official incorporation of the Whitworth Institute. How this came about and why this honour should befall an artist whose fall from critical esteem was so swift and complete that only a few years later the work was placed (like p.72) on indefinite loan to the City Art Gallery, tells us much about the aims of the early founding fathers of the Gallery.

Central to the story was Sir William Agnew who, as the main organiser of the 1887 Manchester Royal Jubilee Exhibition and a prominent member of the Whitworth Committee, was influential in Manchester art circles. Watts was represented at the Jubilee exhibition by no less than thirty-four works (including a version of *Love and Death*). It is clear that for Agnew and his contemporaries Watts represented the highest aspirations of serious public art, the ideal starting point for the Institute's activities. Agnew offered £3000 for the painting and, although Watts declined, he was subsequently persuaded of the seriousness of the venture, so much so that he gave the work as "a sign of being in fellowship with the movement you and your colleagues are instituting".

That Watts' work was already out of date, even in 1887, is hinted at in some of the criticism of the exhibition and emerges strongly from the very defensive notes that he produced to accompany a group of drawings, also acquired by the Institute. "The endeavour", he wrote, "is to identify Art with the best in the conscience and action of the age... to give... expression to the direction of modern thought upon the great problems that have reference to human, spiritual, and moral nature; and with a purposed avoidance of symbols relating to special creeds, or any theological inference." For Watts "Symbolism affords the only means of dealing with abstractions" such as "Life, Death, Faith, Hope, Love, Error, Nemesis"; though as he admits "any Art approaching in appearance the symbolic or didactic, will be generally visited with pronounced disapprobation".

The work had its origins in a portrait commission of the eighth Marquess of Lothian, begun in 1862. It was the long struggle against death by the young Marquess which suggested the idea of illustrating what Watts called "the progress of inevitable, but not terrible death, partially but not completely overshadowing love". Love is shown as a winged youth of indeterminate sex, brushed aside by the cloaked and gigantic figure of Death as she enters a doorway. Around her the roses, that once framed the door, have already collapsed and begun to wither. But this is no *memento mori*. *Love and Death* was designed as an image of consolation for an age that had to face death as an intrusive presence into everyday life, even though its richer members could choose to commemorate their dead through works of art and memorials which used symbolism to cloak the awful reality. Watts' attitude was typical of a certain sort of evasion; he called death "that kind nurse who puts us all as her children to bed."

That Watts answered a deeply felt need for a secular consolation for the meaningless death of a gifted youth is suggested by the number of versions that he produced at least eight; the first was begun in 1868-9. It appears that the Whitworth version, one of the largest, was exhibited at the Grosvenor Gallery in 1877. In the letter to Agnew, Watts explained that he had "worked constantly on it... since 1877, not in the way of making experiments upon it and alterations, but by improving its workmanship and details". In a number of areas the Whitworth version is incomplete and it would appear that the artist did not take it any further. Constant revision certainly explains the muddied coloration of the work, a feature that is also partly explained by the artist's reverence for discoloured Old Master paintings.

Though few would deny that the painting is a fascinating social document, especially for our understanding of Victorian attitudes towards death, it is difficult now to fully appreciate the enthusiasm of its early admirers. Among these was D.H. Lawrence who took Watts' image a stage further, and talked of death as a "dark embracing mother, who slops over us, and frightens us because we are children". GS

Fortifications
of Paris with Houses 1887

Vincent Van Gogh (1853-1890) Dutch

Watercolour and gouache over black chalk, heightened with pencil 395 x 535 mm

Presented by Sir Thomas Barlow in 1927 (D.4.1927)

Van Gogh arrived in Paris in March 1886 and stayed for two years. Sometime during the early Summer of 1887 he began work on a group of drawings in mixed media with the ring of Paris' fortifications as the subject. The artist's motives behind the choice are not known but this drawing, both singly and as part of the group, offers interesting clues to his stylistic concerns at this time and also demonstrate his commitment to a particular sort of modern urban subject matter.

The group of drawings to which the Whitworth sheet is related includes three highly worked views of the fortifications (probably near the Porte de Clichy in the North West of the city), as well as two further drawings, in a similar medium, of subjects in the same area. The drawings are based on three pencil sketches all from the same sketch book. Van Gogh used a complex and unusual technique and one that was almost certainly studio based. The initial underdrawing, based on the sketches, was in black chalk, over which the artist worked in broad touches of watercolour and gouache. Finally he used pencil to pick out further details, adding pastel to increase the range of textural effects. The colours are bright and unmixed showing the use of complementary colours which was such an important part of the palette of those younger artists in Paris associated with the *avant garde* camp. The use of mixed media in this way, with the juxtaposition of broad touches of colour, suggests that the artist may initially have had an oil painting in mind. One of the limitations of watercolour is also apparent in the foreground, namely, the difficulty of correcting mistakes, for one can still clearly see the ghost of two figures which the artist has tried to paint out.

The subject of the Paris fortifications was a common one for artists during the 1880s. They had been built between 1841 and 1845 and consisted of a series of bastions, gates and forts linked by a wall with a ditch on the outside. As a defensive system it had been a spectacular failure during the Franco-Prussian War and there had been calls for its removal. The walls seemed to many to act as an unnecessary barrier to urban expansion and since the fortifications flanked many of the poorest areas it not surprisingly attracted a reputation as a place of vice and violence, especially at night. But there was another aspect of the situation, one that was more relevant to Van Gogh. A side effect of the need for open spaces around the fortifications for defensive reasons, was the provision of land in highly populated areas for the lower classes, particularily on Sunday, to relax and stroll. It is this rather than the more violent associations that the artist chose to stress.

The suburb, that faceless no-man's-land between the city proper and the country, was a particular concern of *avant garde* artists during this period. Van Gogh, in earlier city views painted in Holland and in Paris, had turned his back on the gregarious sites of middle-class pleasure and the great set pieces of the historical capital and concentrated on depicting scenes that were profoundly ordinary. Here he may well have been inspired by the strong diagonal created by the man-made barrier, a compositional device that recurs throughout his career but it is the remorselessly ordinary nature of the scene that catches the eye. This is city life shorn of all of its consolations and excitement; it is portrayed by an outsider, someone who was just passing through and is uncertain of his position in the vast sprawling impersonal city.

GS

Femme au lit, profil—Au petit lever 1896

(Woman in bed, profile—Waking up)
Plate from Elles (Women)
Henri de Toulouse-Lautrec (1864-1901) French
Printed by Auguste Clot; published by Gustave Pellet
Crayon, brush and spatter lithograph with scraper; printed in four colours; sheet size 402 x 518 mm
Purchased in 1930 (5130)

The image used on the cover and frontispiece of the series *Elles* from which this print is taken would seem to announce the subject matter of the ten colour lithographs which make up the set. The title *Elles* translates literally as 'They' in the feminine gender, and the cover shows a back view of a woman doing her hair, her clothes strewn around her, and the dark shape of a man's top hat placed prominently in the foreground, indicating the presence of this prostitute's male client. Toulouse-Lautrec is known to have visited Parisian brothels, especially during the 1890s, when he would even take the unusual step of renting a room in a brothel for some time, living almost as 'one of the family' and deliberately shocking dealers and colleagues by giving the name of the brothel as his business address. It has recently been suggested, however, that the subject of *Elles* is really the daily life of a lesbian couple, although it would still seem that they made their living by prostitution, since objects such as the top hat and the mythological paintings of erotic subjects in some of the scenes would have indicated prostitutes and their clients to Toulouse-Lautrec's contemporary audiences.

Whatever its precise subject, there is a notable lack of eroticism in Toulouse-Lautrec's handling of the images in the series. None of the women is shown naked, or in suggestive poses; instead, Lautrec has focussed on the mundane aspects of their everyday life—eating meals, getting dressed, washing, doing their hair,—all presented without a hint of glamour or excitement. The idea of producing such a series may have come from Japanese prints, such as Utamaro's *The 12 Hours of the Green Houses* (brothels were known in Japan as 'green houses'). Certainly the style of some of Toulouse-Lautrec's work with its combination of areas of flat pattern with others treated in great detail, shows his debt to Japanese prints; a debt he acknowledges in his monogram in the lower left corner, which was designed to look like a Japanese seal. The idea for the series might also have been suggested by its publisher, Gustave Pellet, since he was well known for

his preference for erotic or even pornographic subject matter. However, if this were the case, Pellet may well have been disappointed by the lack of erotic excitement in Lautrec's images; indeed Pellet's relationship with Lautrec was broken off only a couple of years after the publication of *Elles*. Lautrec clearly preferred to study the lives of these women in a quieter way, producing images which contain no moral or social criticism of their lives and activities.

Some of Toulouse-Lautrec's contemporaries were torn between their admiration for his obvious technical skills as a draughtsman and printmaker, and their dislike of what they considered to be his 'vice-ridden' subject matter. The series *Elles* has long been admired as a great technical achievement, even though Lautrec employed but a limited number of the wide range of lithographic techniques available to him. He tended to use only one type of lithographic crayon, and hardly ever used a pen, preferring instead a brush, as on the crimson bedspread here, with a scraper to take out highlights. Perhaps the technique for which he is now best known, although he did not actually invent it, is 'crachis' (literally 'to spit') or 'spatter'. This involves dipping a short haired brush into lithographic ink, then running the blade of a knife over the bristles to produce a fine rain of ink, such as those used for the wallpaper and bed-spread on this plate, or (in multiple colours) on the standing woman's hair. Paper stencils were used to mask out areas not to be treated in this way.

The publisher Pellet was known for the luxuriousness of his publications, and *Elles* certainly did not sell cheaply—the set cost 300 francs, or 35 for each individual print, whereas Lautrec's posters could be as cheap as 1 fr 50 or 5 fr each. No trouble or expense was spared in the production of the lithographs; the paper itself was made especially for the project, with both Pellet's and Lautrec's names in the watermark, whilst the large number of surviving trial proofs clearly show the great care taken with the printing.   SH

Poverty 1903
Pablo Ruiz Picasso (1881-1973) Spanish

Pen and ink and wash 375 x 267 mm
Presented by A.E. Anderson in 1928 (D.40.1928)
©DACS 1988

Picasso painted this work in Barcelona in 1903 in the middle of what has subsequently been called the Blue Period. The artist had begun to restrict his palette in 1901, when he was still in Paris, and its dominance was to last until his full time return to France in 1904. The use of a single colour, monochrome in its true sense, was accompanied by a new range of subject matter very different from the bright scenes of cafe and city life that Picasso had produced earlier in his stay in Paris. Concentrating on a restricted range of characters, a cast of beggars, impoverished family groups, blind people, and lonely individuals, the artist produced numerous moving images of human suffering, of people driven to the edges of society. Though there is no sense of communication between individuals in these works, no spark of life or rebellion, the figures do still retain some shreds of human dignity amongst all the suffering. The scale of the figures, their dogged resilience and, in this work, the way that they continue to move forward whilst keeping together as a family group, often mitigate against an entirely pessimistic reading. In *Poverty* there is even a hint of a religious parallel which is not untypical of the period; the family group bears a number of resemblances to the traditional depictions of the Holy Family on the Flight into Egypt.

Why Picasso should choose to turn to such subjects at this particular point in his career and why he should use such a restricted palette, are closely related. Certainly the use of blue, traditionally associated with melancholy, is in keeping with the subject matter. It also reflects the influence of Symbolists like Puvis de Chavannes, whose images of lonely individuals such as *Solitude* (the drawing for which is in the Gallery's collection) also used a very restricted colour range. A lack of colour denies the viewer the consolation of surface attractions which could distract from a proper response to the subject. The blue background also has the effect of removing the work from any specific context; what is created is a universal, timeless image of suffering in which the actual causes of poverty, social or economic, are excluded.

For a number of writers, however, Picasso's subjects of this period seem to reflect not so much a new social awareness but rather a period of personal upheaval and depression subsequent to the death of his companion, and close friend, Casagemas. Such ideas are however purely hypothetical, and in concentrating on the individual miss the point that, as with Van Gogh (p.94), the subject matter is almost as important as the style in defining the artist's position towards the mainstream of art production. Picasso's shift, in four years, from scenes of urban nightlife to the outcasts and victims of society and finally the characteristic images of the Rose Period, the clowns and Harlequins, show a restless curiosity about those who live at the edges of society, the outsiders, that is just as modern in its implications as the style employed.   GS

Peacock Frieze

Designed by W. Dennington British

Manufactured by Shand Kydd Ltd, 1900
Portion of a wallpaper frieze, colour print from wood blocks 838 x 1041 mm
Presented by Crown Wallcoverings Ltd in 1987 (W.298.1987)

The fashion for deep wallpaper friezes was well-established in artistic circles by the mid-1890s and these decorations, particularly those with a hand block-printed outline enclosing stencilled colours, remained popular for the next decade. They varied in depth and longitudinal repeat and employed a wide range of subject matter including allegorical and classical scenes, naturalistic landscape effects, and exotic flowers and foliage. One critic suggested that, in order to get "the true and undisturbed value" of the designer's imagination, the dimensions of these decorations might usefully be increased to 30 inches or even 40 inches deep. Although comparatively highly priced, their popularity was widespread and they were described as being "somewhat brilliant in colour". It is therefore not surprising that the frieze tended to be used in conjunction with a plain tinted or textured wallpaper filling from which it was separated by a moulded picture rail.

A large number of these productions were manufactured by William Shand Kydd and contemporary accounts suggest that it was to him that the style owed its considerable popularity "in the very best class of houses". A Scot, Shand Kydd had come to London in the early 1880s. He had worked for Hayward & Son, who were credited with having re-introduced and pioneered the use of stencilling in modern wallpapers. And it is likely that he developed his own ideas for combining hand block printing and stencilling during this period, including the blending of several colours into one ground. Subsequently, with the establishment of his own business in Marylebone Road in 1891, his reputation for the design and manufacture of blocked and stencilled patterns increased until his products were said to be "in the front rank of the artistic wallpapers of the day".

This example, in so far as it employs the characteristic technique of a block-printed outline and stencilled, blended colours, is typical of the friezes issued by Shand Kydd during the first decade of the twentieth century. However, it is not one of his own designs which, for the most part, employed the swirling, curvilinear shapes and organic motifs associated with the Art Nouveau style. Although it features the strong, jewel-like colours which were a hallmark of his decorations, this frieze, depicting a peacock superimposed on a stylised arrangement of climbing roses, is rather restrained in style and static in feeling; it resembles a stained glass window rather than an exotic garden. It was designed by W. Dennington of whom, unfortunately, little is known except that s/he designed at least one other frieze for the firm and was able, as was Shand Kydd himself, to interpret 'modern tendencies' for the popular market. This design reflects the influences of decorative art of the preceding twenty years, and different strands of the Aesthetic movement, Art Nouveau, and Arts and Crafts are all apparent in a diluted form. Interestingly, it was chosen by the Arts and Crafts architect Hugh Baillie Scott as part of the decorative scheme of Blackwell School, in Cumberland, where it has survived in the hall since the turn of the century.   CW

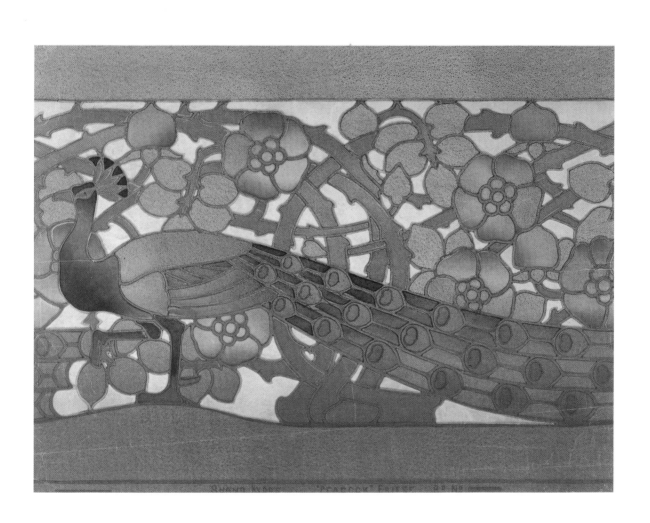

Fool's Parsley 1907

Designed by Charles Francis Annesley Voysey (1857-1941) British

Design for a wallpaper, pencil and watercolour 762 x 559 mm

Presented by The Wall Paper Manufacturers Ltd in 1967 (W.63.1967)

Although he was described by *The Studio* as "an architect first and foremost", C.F.A. Voysey's achievement and influence in the sphere of decorative art was considerable. Having trained under the architect and furniture designer J.P. Seddon, he set up his own practice in the early 1880s and, whilst waiting for commissions, began to design wallpaper and textiles. He was encouraged in this venture by his architect friend A.H. Mackmurdo who had designed a number of papers for Jeffrey & Co, and it was this firm that produced Voysey's first designs.

By 1890 he was designing for most of the leading wallpaper manufacturers, and, by the turn of the century, his work was widely known both in Europe and the U.S.A. largely because his considerable output for Essex & Co was so much publicised.

The early designs show the influence of Mackmurdo's boldly curvaceous swirling style and can be seen to reflect some of the characteristics of 'Art Nouveau,' a manifestation which, paradoxically, Voysey abhorred—he described it in 1904 as "distinctly unhealthy and revolting". He was also out of sympathy with the socialist ideals of William Morris and disliked the sensuality of his work. But nevertheless Voysey's stylisation of nature owed much both to Morris' influence and to the romanticism of the English Arts and Crafts movement. However, by the 1890s, the geometry which characterised his architecture had become more dominant in his wallpaper designs, rendering them more spacious and delicate. They had developed a lightness of touch and whimsical approach that was all Voysey's own and which reflected his interest in vernacular design.

Indeed, he prized individuality above almost everything else. He saw it as essential that individual creativity be preserved in the face of the "arrogant demon of Commercialism"—a creature he appears to have tamed by developing a relationship based on close co-operation with a number of manufacturers, in particular Essex & Co. This enabled him to maintain a degree of control over the finished product which was (and is) unusual for the

British industrial designer, and has resulted in his work being described as "an extraordinary instance of commercial application of a highly personalised vision".

By 1896 'Voysey wallpaper' was said to be as well known as 'Morris chintz' or 'Liberty silk', but his output dropped substantially after 1900 and he developed a sparser, more naive style, which was in dramatic contrast to his earlier rather lush, sophisticated patterns.

Fool's Parsley is typical of the later papers, exhibiting the simple airy elegance which characterised his work and making no attempt to disguise the structure of the design repeat. In common with the majority of his designs, it features stylised plant forms and also incorporates the ubiquitous formalised bird motifs for which he is best known. Arguing that, when conventionally treated, the bird is "merely a flat symbol", he called for the breaking down of the "unreasonable, unhealthy and insane" opposition to the application of animal life to decoration. He agreed that the realistic treatment of birds had "very properly been denounced as a painful spectacle" when plastered around angles or cut in half by cornices, but he could not accept that the symbol of a bird was more problematic than the symbol of a flower. Bemoaning what he perceived as a lack of delight in bird-life, he remarked that the public only associated birds with "the shooting season and bread sauce".

Fool's Parsley was produced by Arthur Sanderson & Sons Ltd in 1907, for whom, in addition to wallpapers, graphics and metalwork, Voysey also designed his only factory building, built in 1903.

It is ironic that, having probably exercised as much influence on designers and decorators as Morris, Voysey's own design work did not develop significantly after the turn of the century, although he continued to design wallpapers until 1930. F.G. Froggatt, reviewing new papers in 1908, lamented that "the papers show no marked departure from those of previous years. Mr Voysey remains faithful to his birds". CW

Church and Dove c1925

Designed by Edward Bawden (b.1903) British

Printed by the Curwen Press
Hand-printed wallpaper, colour lithograph 564 x 545mm
Presented by the artist in 1987 (W.315.1987)

Born in 1903, Edward Bawden's long and highly productive career has spanned many different spheres of artistic activity. He is perhaps best-known today for his work as a landscape artist and book illustrator but his prolific output has also included mural paintings, advertisments, poster designs, decorations for ceramics and printed textiles and, most recently, designs for garden furniture. Given the obvious breadth of his interests it is not altogether surprising that Bawden should have turned his attention to the production of wallpapers as well. He designed approximately thirty patterns, all between the years 1925 and 1939, and although numerically they represent a comparatively small proportion of his *oeuvre*, they comprise one of its most attractive and idiosyncratic constituents.

Church and Dove was the first of Bawden's wallpapers and was produced when he was still a student at the Royal College of Art in 1925. It was originally printed in oil colours from lino-cuts in what was, by all accounts, a somewhat eccentric and haphazard way. P.D.Bliss, Bawden's biographer and friend, recalls how Bawden pressed out the pattern with his feet onto rolls of lining paper that were laid out on the floor of his tiny studio in Redcliffe Gardens, Chelsea. Clearly, this particular brand of cottage industry could not sustain production on any significant scale and the manufacture of the wallpaper was taken over shortly afterwards by the Curwen Press. Harold Curwen, the firm's proprietor, had the design transferred to a lithographic plate and it was printed on small sheets that measured approximately 24 inches square. It was then sold exclusively through the Knightsbridge shop, Modern Textiles, and retailed at the comparatively high price of 2s a piece. Whether prospective customers were deterred by the cost or by the potential difficulties of hanging small sheets of this size is unclear, but the design did not sell well and Bawden's royalties amounted to no more than £2 0s 10d after six years!

Visually, however, *Church and Dove* has enormous appeal. Oliver Simon, the artistic director of the Curwen Press, described it as "subtle, fresh and beautiful" and in relation to other productions of the period it stands out as strikingly individual and unusual. It resembles neither the modernist offerings of the Bauhaus school with their minimalist flecked and textured effects, nor more conventional designs which consisted in the main of large floral and foliate motifs. In fact, the most useful comparison is with certain wallpapers of the Victorian age. William Morris was a particularly important influence on Bawden; it was apparently the discovery of his *Daisy* pattern that first awakened the younger artist's interest in wallpapers and the simplicity and unpretentiousness of Morris's work is echoed in the 'homely' motifs and deliberately naive style of his own design.

Church and Dove survives today in Bawden's home where it has been used to decorate the hallway and stairs. The colours have faded a little over the years but a recent Bawden watercolour of the interior of the house has recaptured and preserved all the original freshness of the design.   JB

Animals marching into the Ark 1927

Plate from The Chester Play of The Deluge
Designed and engraved by David Jones (1895-1974) British

Printed by A.C. Cooper; published by the Golden Cockerel Press.
Wood engraving; image size 165 x 143 mm
Presented by Margaret Pilkington in 1960 (5991)

David Jones' wood engraving illustrates a scene in a play from one of the four surviving versions of the complete English Mystery Cycle of plays, known as the Chester Cycle. Each individual play, such as *The Deluge*, was an episode from the complete cycle which, performed annually, was the highlight of the year in the community life of many medieval English towns. The Cycle presented a history of the world from the Creation to the Last Judgement, the central mystical events being the birth, death and resurrection of Christ. *The Deluge* tells the story of Noah, who was instructed by God to build an ark against a coming deluge, and to take on board animals and birds with which to populate the earth again once the flood waters had receded. This particular print illustrates the lines,

> *And heare are beares, woulfes sette*
> *Apes, oules, marmosette,*
> *Weyscelles, squirelles, and firrette,*
> *Heare the eaten ther meate.*
>
> *And heare are fowles lesse and more,*
> *Hearnes, cranes, and byttour,*
> *Swannes, peacokes and them before*
> *Meate for this weither.*

The illustration of a play such as this held an obvious appeal for someone like David Jones, whose work as an artist was inextricably bound up with his religious beliefs. Jones was born into a devout Anglican family but his experiences in the trenches during the First World War contributed to his conversion to the Roman Catholic faith in 1921. In that year, on leaving art school, he became a postulant in a craft guild—the Guild of St Joseph and St Dominic. This community of Dominican tertiaries had been founded at Ditchling few years earlier by Hilary Pepler and Eric Gill as a religious fraternity "for those who wanted to make things with their hands". On his arrival Jones was set to work as a carpenter, making looms

weaving which was evidently Gill's way of knocking any 'aesthetic nonsense' out of the head of a young art student. He also began to learn how to engrave on wood, the technique he was to use for these illustrations to *The Deluge*.

At the time an interest in this particular printmaking process was unusual since etching and lithography were the main techniques fashionable with art students. However, the guild of St Joseph and St Dominic was to be a pioneering force in the revival of wood engraving in England during the 1920s. Eric Gill's encouragement of the craft had as much to do with the qualities it encouraged in its practitioners as with the qualities of the final printed images: "The advantage of wood engraving", he wrote, "is that it does away with several sets of middle men and places responsibility on the shoulders of the workman. The workman who draws, engraves and prints his own blocks is master of the situation." Jones too realized that he could learn much from wood engraving: "the discipline of engraving—of doing jobs however badly, the sharpening of tools, and the atmosphere of workshop rather than of studio, and the clarifying ideas of Mr Gill were at that time, and for me, of very great value".

Jones became very closely involved with the Gill family, moving with them in 1924 from Ditchling to the Black Mountains, north of Abergavenny, where the Gills lived in the former monastery at Capel-y-Ffin. From here Jones made excursions to Caldy Island where, in the early months of 1927, he stayed with a group of Benedictine monks who allowed him to use their scriptorium to work at his wood engraving; it was probably here that he began work on the illustrations for *The Deluge*. Altogether the ten plates seem to have taken him the best part of a year to complete. The work was commissioned and published by The Golden Cockerel Press, a private press founded in 1920 by Harold Taylor. Jones was one of a number of artists, who contributed towards their finely made editions in the tradition of those produced by Morris at the Kelmscott Press (see p.88). SH

E.20.   Illustration to Bethya

David Jones

37

John Deth
(Hommage à Conrad Aiken) 1931

Edward Burra (1905-1976) British

Gouache over pencil 671 x 1026 mm

Purchased in 1982 with the aid of grants from the Victoria and Albert Museum
Purchase Grant Fund and the National Art-Collections Fund (D.8.1982)

Burra met the American poet Conrad Aiken for the first time in 1931 and quickly established a long lasting and deep friendship. They were introduced by a mutual friend, the artist Paul Nash, and it was he who suggested to the publishers Cassells that they produce a new edition by Burra of Aiken's poem *John Deth*, written in 1922-24, illustrated by Burra. The project, unfortunately, came to nothing and this watercolour is all that remains of what would have been a lasting memorial or *hommage*, as the subtitle suggests, to a poet of the first rank from a close friend and colleague who had found in Aiken's work many echoes of his own ideas.

The drawing illustrates section seven of part one, the scene at the Star-Tree Inn where Deth is mingling with the revellers. Although the following quotation contains the substance of the drawing there is also much that is clearly Burra's own invention.

> *The fiddlers struck the buzzing strings,*
> *And sang, and nodded polished skulls,*
> *While round them frolicked the frumps and trulls.*
> *The Bishop passed them with a caper,*
> *Waving aloft a learned paper.*
> *Behind him tripped the sad-eyed vicar*
> *Who beamed on Millicent...*
> *"Come, Millicent, my spangled queen!*
> *Come thump your shivering tambourine-*
> *And dance me to the realm unseen!"*
> *But Millicent gave his arm a shove:*
> *"No, no! it's not the dead I love!"*

Knowing that Aiken was inspired by Holbein's painting *The Dance of Death*, Burra has chosen to show John Deth as a skeleton, cloaked in scarlet and carrying a scythe, who creeps up behind his victims. In the poem Deth easily triumphs over the revellers who include representatives of a contemporary society that both Burra and Aiken felt to be hollow, superficial and, in the Freudian sense, possessed of an unhealthy collective death wish. The point which Burra chose to illustrate occurs when Millicent, who symbolizes positive, life enhancing qualities repels Death (Deth) in all his power.

Burra's vision of a hellish party owes much to his knowledge of the work of a wide range of other artists. The most obvious debt is to the twentieth-century German artist George Grosz. Burra makes use of the same range of strident and unnatural colours to capture the raucous noise and wild confusion of the decadent lifestyle of his contemporaries. The figures are also distorted and exaggerated in ways similar to those used by Grosz to expose the immorality of post-war German society. It is not surprising that Burra used this work to represent him at a number of the most important exhibitions of Surrealism as, aside from its recreation of a horrific nightmare, it displays the artist's unnerving ability to transform familiar detail into something disturbing and strange. But perhaps no less important, certainly in convincing us that there is a moral point to the work, is its close allegiance to English satirical prints of the eighteenth century. This is true both of its compositional structure and of its use of a social gathering in a place of recreation, to point to the sickness which lies barely hidden below the surface of the polite mask. Surrealist distortions here perform the same function as caricature did for the political cartoonists and moralists of the earlier period.

GS

Dame à la Huppe (Woman of Means) 1939

Plate from Passion by André Suarès
Designed and etched by Georges Rouault (1871-1958) French

Printed by Roger Lacourière; published by Ambrose Vollard
Aquatint, printed in colours; page size 440 x 340 mm
Presented by Margaret Pilkington in 1948 (5499)
©DACS 1988

It will come as no surprise that the designer of this print, Georges Rouault, was apprenticed at the age of fourteen to a stained glass maker, and later worked for a restorer of historic stained glass. The firm black outlines of his image set off the bright, almost translucent coloured inks, in much the same way as the black lead supports and enlivens the coloured areas of a stained glass window. Rouault has been described as "the outstanding religious artist of the twentieth century". He was trained as a painter under Gustave Moreau at the École des Beaux Arts in Paris during the 1890s, and took up printmaking around 1910, remaining preoccupied with it for many years, and achieving striking effects by quite unorthodox means. Many of his finest prints, including this one, were issued as book illustrations.

Like many of the prints included in this publication, *Dame à la Huppe* is by no means the work of a single artist. The skills of the printer, Roger Lacourière, and the organisational abilities of the publisher, Ambrose Vollard, were equally important, as were the ideas of the writer, André Suarès, whose dramatic narrative of Christ's Passion provided the starting point for the images.

The ideas and enthusiasm of the publisher, Vollard, provided vital encouragement for Rouault, although their relationship was not always easy; Rouault often despaired at the endless delays that Vollard's indecision caused. However, their relationship lasted for 33 years; *Passion* was in fact the last book which Vollard saw completed and issued during his lifetime—he died in 1939, only a few months after its publication.

Although Vollard had begun his career as an art dealer, the business into which he poured most of the income he gained was the publication of fine prints, and books illustrated by 'peintre-graveurs' (painter-engravers)—that is, artists who were not professional printmakers by training. His main concern in publishing such books was with the visual appearance of the volumes. He was prepared to go to endless lengths to find the right paper, the most suitable typography, the best size of margin, and of course the right artist to produce the illustration. In this he was fully supported by associates such as the printer Georges Aubert, who even designed a special press on which to print wood engravings after drawings by Rouault; Rouault in turn was prepared to experiment endlessly with new techniques in order to produce his striking images. As a later critic was to write, this work involved using "almost every instrument known to the engraver and every acid known to the etcher in order to render to his satisfaction the tones and values of his unique images". The combination of this and of Vollard's high standards of production resulted in the spectacular, lectern-sized *edition de luxe* of Suarès' *Passion*. Of it Vollard is said to have remarked: "Books like these have never been done before and will never be done again". SH

At the Coal Face 1942

Henry Moore (1898-1986) British

Wax crayons with grey wash, pen and ink and surface scratching 334 x 551 mm

Presented by the War Artists' Advisory Commission in 1947 (D.37.1947)

Artists during the Second World War faced a number of economic problems which, in the case of sculptors, were compounded by shortages of materials. The War Artists' Advisory Commission was able to help many artists and to provide commissions to record various aspects of the war, ranging from the Home Front and industrial production through to the soldier's life on active service. In a number of cases, including Moore's, they introduced the artist to new subject matter which was to be of lasting benefit.

Moore's first commission had been to record scenes in the London Underground at the height of the Blitz, but by the end of 1941 he had begun to search for a new project. It was suggested that he should combine his interest in life underground with his own family background in a Yorkshire mining village and work on a group of studies of coal miners, "Britain's Underground Army", as wartime propaganda put it. Moore requested, and was granted, permission to visit the Wheldale Colliery, Castleford, where his father had been a miner, and the town where he had been brought up.

Moore's first visit down a mine was an overwhelming experience; he was later to record that, "If one were asked to describe what Hell might be like, this would do. A dense darkness you could touch, the whirring din of the coal-cutting machine, throwing into the air black dust so thick that the light beams from the miners' lamps could only shine into it a few inches—the impresssion of numberless short pit-props placed only a foot or two apart, to support above them a mile's weight of rock and earth ceiling—all this in the stifling heat. I have never had a tougher day in my life".

In the first few days Moore was content just to observe the miners at work, the drama of the caves and tunnels, and the strange geometry of the pit-props and railway lines. He then began to sketch, producing numerous drawings to various degrees of finish, in three sketch books. Apart from the shock of discovering the nature of life under-ground, Moore was also surprised by his own artistic response. "I had never willingly drawn male figures before... But here... I discovered the male figure and the qualities of the figure in action. As a sculptor I had previously believed only in static forms, that is, forms in repose." Movement in such a restricted space was mainly confined to the upper body. The figure in the Whitworth drawing seems to be pivoted at the waist, the sweeping movement placing all the emphasis on the miner's back.

After a fortnight studying and sketching underground, Moore returned to the studio. In the following six months he produced some twenty large drawings, using the same complex mixed media of pen and ink, chalk, wax crayon and watercolour which he had used in the London Underground drawings. The media was a direct response to the specific problems of the commission: "In the coal-mine drawings, a special problem was to show the black smudges of coal dust on the miners' faces, and at the same time show the shape, the form beneath the black smudges, that is, one was using the same chalk or pencil to do two things, to show colour and form together, without confusion or contradiction". Taking hints from the work of artists as diverse as Rembrandt and the drawings of Seurat, Moore included in the work the source of light and it is this which gives to the major figure in particular, its sculptural massiveness. Reversing the traditional relationship in a drawing between the white ground and the dark mark made, Moore worked from dark to light in order to recreate a sense of "that dense darkness".

At The Coal Face is typical of the group in that figures remain impersonalised. But Moore stops short of reducing the figures to animal forms, crushed by the hardships of their labour and the unnaturalness of the location. There is a sense of the heroic in the main figure, his broad back supporting "a mile's weight of rock" above yet remaining unbowed; his contribution to the war effort less equivocal than that of a "mere" artist.   GS

Reclining Figure 1948

Designed by Henry Moore (1898-1986) British

Manufactured by Ascher (London) Limited
Screen-printed linen 1830 x 2640 mm
Purchased in 1961 (T.10253)

Lida and Zika Ascher, both natives of Prague, were on honeymoon in 1939 when Czechoslovakia was annexed by the Nazis. They fled to London where they set up a small business selling, and eventually manufacturing, fashion fabrics. Just before the end of the war, Zika Ascher began to approach leading artists of the day to design head squares and dress fabrics for him.

Henry Moore was one of the first artists with whom the Aschers worked. The collaboration, which began in 1944, was highly successful, and his designs were printed as yardage for dress fabrics as well as squares. The large linen wall-hanging, *Reclining Figure*, was one of four such panels which represented Ascher's most ambitious project to date. Along with a further design by Moore, *Two Standing Figures*, and two by Matisse, the panels were shown at the Lefevre Gallery in London in the autumn of 1948 and were then toured in Britain and abroad.

The Ascher panels were a logical progression from the squares, which had been marketed from the outset as works of art as well as head adornments. The panels were conceived as wall decorations on a grand scale, intended, as the Lefevre catalogue put it, to be "as representative of our age, as the Gobelins and medieval tapestries" had been of their times, and Moore's monumental pictorial designs come fairly close to tapestry conceptions. Each design was printed in a limited edition of thirty, and the panels were individually numbered and signed by the artist.

Moore's designs were difficult to translate on to the cloth, and many months of experimentation were necessary before completely satisfactory results were achieved. Like the squares, the large panels were screen-printed by hand at the Aschers' own printworks, and since Moore's original drawings were executed in wax crayons and watercolour, Ascher used a wax resist technique to print them. The silkscreen had only come into general use in the textile industry in the 1930s, but it offered much greater scope than either woodblocks or rollers for the accurate reproduction of an artist's design and the texture of brushstrokes, and Moore's *Reclining Figure* is full of texture and subtle colour variations. Furthermore, the fact that the silkscreen was an inexpensive technique in comparison with engraved metal rollers made it particularly suitable for small runs of fabric and limited editions.

Henry Moore's designs work surprisingly well as textiles. Even when put into small-scale repeat for squares or dress fabrics his drawings still manage to retain their enormous vigour and characteristic 'handwriting'. His two panels for Ascher were generally well received, although one critic wondered whether their "forcefulness and power" was not too overwhelming for the ordinary domestic interior (Sydney *Sun*, 20 June 1949).

The idea of uniting fine art with industrial production was a popular one in the 1930s and 1940s. Although the British market tended to be more conservative than the continental one in its commitment to modern art and design, a number of more adventurous manufacturers began to approach contemporary artists for designs in the mid-1930s. Amongst them were Allan Walton Textiles (established 1933) who commissioned designs from Duncan Grant and Vanessa Bell, and Edinburgh Weavers, whose Constructivist collection with designs from Ben Nicholson and Barbara Hepworth was launched in 1937. It is in this context that the Aschers' project should be viewed. Artist-designed textiles lent credibility to a rather depressed and uncertain industry, as Norman Bel Geddes, the American industrial designer, wrote in *Horizon* in 1932:

the artist's contribution touches upon that most important of all phases entering into selling, the psychological. He appeals to the consumer's vanity and plays upon his imagination. JH

Portrait of Lucian Freud 1951

Francis Bacon (b.1909) British

Oil on canvas 1980 x 1370 mm

Purchased in 1980 with the aid of grants from the Victoria and Albert Museum
Purchase Grant Fund, the National Art-Collections Fund and
the Friends of the Whitworth (O.3.1980)

This is the first of a series of portraits of Bacon's fellow artist and long time friend, Lucian Freud. The work is particularly important as the first example, in Bacon's career, of a portrait of a named individual and, as such, stands at the beginning of a series of studies of a small group of close friends which has remained a central part of the artist's work. Given the ways in which Bacon distorts the image of his subjects it is easy to see why portraiture has always meant painting understanding and sympathetic friends and not working on a commission. "Who can I tear to pieces if not my friends?" he has asked; "If they were not my friends I could not do such violence to them".

But even if Bacon is confident of a sympathetic response he still prefers to work from photographs without the sitter being present since, as he puts it, "I would rather practise the injury in private by which I think I can record the *facts* of them more clearly". The use of a photograph is important for other reasons too. It means that painting becomes a matter of memory not observation; the portrait is thus a way of bringing back the presence of the sitter. This in turn allows the artist to escape from what he sees as the prosaic fact of reality, in pursuit of other qualities, whilst at the same time not sacrificing a close personal commitment to the subject. Here, as we shall see, a photograph also provides the starting point for the composition.

To understand Bacon's approach to portraiture one needs to consider his definition of the word "fact". The nature of contemporary existence is, in Bacon's eyes, such that "who today has been able to record anything that comes across to us as a *fact* without causing deep injury to the image". The portrait of Freud was painted at time when the notion that an artist could objectively record the facts of a person, within the naturalistic tradition, had been hopelessly compromised; to many of Bacon's contemporaries it required desperate measures to save the portrait from years of flattery and hyperbole. The problem of likeness had also been compounded by photography.

For many artists the question of likeness, in its most limited sense, had been taken care of and the challenge was to go a stage further. In Bacon's work this usually meant painting from a photograph and working in ways that disrupted the mechanical and slick representation of the subject.

This disruption could take a number of forms. Here Bacon leaves part of the foreground as bare canvas: the lack of finish serving to underline the artifice of the whole. Likewise he is also happy to incorporate elements of chance into the work. In this case splashes of paint in the foreground and the careless way in which the frame encloses the figure contrast with the highly worked up areas around the face. We do however, need to be careful that we don't bring to this painting our knowledge of Bacon's later, more extreme distortions; it is easy to miss the point that if taken in isolation, much of this work, in particular the face, is closely related to the Old Master tradition and specifically to the late work of Rembrandt. Bacon is thus able to take a very traditional format—the life size, full-length portrait—and to disrupt our expectations.

There is one further area which must be considered and that is the derivation of Freud's pose from a photograph of the writer Franz Kafka which Bacon knew from the frontispiece to Max Brod's biography. The photograph shows the young writer, dressed in a suit, leaning against a column. Bacon uses this pose with little change; other features such as the shadow behind Freud, the column to the right, as well as the suggestion of the door, all have their origins in this image. Whether the artist simply intended to borrow a pose for its formal implications or if he meant to develop a parallel between the existentialist novelist Kafka and Freud, the archetypal drifting, rootless artist, is not certain. But the knowledge of such a possibility helps to strengthen the sense of unease created by the image, enhanced by the encroachment of two shadows into the foreground of the picture.   GS

Ancoats Hospital Outpatients' Hall 1952

Lawrence Stephen Lowry (1887-1976) British

Oil on canvas 593 x 900 mm

Presented by the Ancoats Hospital Medical Committee in 1975 (O.3.1975)

This rather uncharacteristic work by Lowry was painted in 1952 as a commission for Ancoats Hospital Medical Committee in memory of P.G. McEvedy, Senior Surgeon at the hospital. A minute for January 1953 records that the cost of the commission was £200; how the money to pay the artist's fee came to be available in the first place is in itself a story worth recounting. The immediate source was money paid by the Lancashire Educational Authority to the Hospital Medical Board for operations carried out for the removal of tonsils, this being in the days before the National Health Service and when Ancoats Hospital was one of many charity status hospitals in the area. The money left over at the time of the hospital's incorporation into the National Health Service, was divided between those doctors who had worked in the hospital in an honorary capacity and the Hospital Board, who used their share for general good works of which the McEvedy memorial painting was one example.

Perhaps because the painting is a rare example of a commissioned work, Lowry seems to have taken particular care over its completion. The artist first produced an on-the-spot study in pencil, chalk and watercolour, in which only a few of the figures bear more than a passing resemblance to the final work. Lowry also used a photograph of the interior, to help him fix the details of the architecture. The gap between the drawing and the final painting suggests that, like his more characteristic works, the figures, if not the setting, come from the imagination or from his repertoire of figure types. Whilst the figures in the sketch go busily on their way, quite faceless and certainly unaware of the artist's gaze, in the final painting many of them face the artist/audience as in a more traditional commission where the subjects are required to pose for the artist.

It is easy to miss or ignore some of the horrific details which often intrude into the work of an artist who, in the public imagination, is often reduced to the level of cosy industrial nostalgia. In fact one of the most unusual features of this work is the complete absence of any suffering or hardship in a subject that might, we suppose, have encouraged the artist to indulge in morbid curiosity that is such a feature of his work. In *The Cripples*, also in the Whitworth, the savage caricatures verge on the cruel. But here, perhaps inhibited by the commission, the artist has produced a consoling image in which all the occupants of the waiting room happily pose for the camera.

The Outpatients' Hall has remained essentially unaltered since 1952.   GS

Got a Girl 1960-61

Peter Blake (b.1932) British

Enamel, photo collage and record 920 x 1530 mm

Purchased in 1976 with a grant from the Victoria and Albert Museum
Purchase Grant Fund (O.3.1976)

The title of this work comes from a song by the Four Preps; the record, which was released in 1960, is included as a collage element in the top left corner. The lyrics of the song describe the frustrations of a boy whose girlfriend is much more interested in her heroes than him; whenever he wants to kiss her all she can think of are the pop stars whose pictures are featured in the work. They are, from left to right: Fabian, Frankie Avalon, Ricky Nelson, Bobby Rydell and two of Elvis Presley. The images are taken from magazines; crudely printed and on poor quality paper they have faded and mellowed, as is the fate of such ephemeral objects, and, in a way also that rather fortuitously suggests the passing of time and the memory of the heroes of one's youth.

The lower part of the work reflects the artist's interest in another sort of pop culture, folk art, the popular culture of the past which, by survival to the present day, can represent a similar alternative to the closed tradition of Fine Art as contemporary throwaway culture. What at first seems to be an abstract painting, based on a simple chevron pattern turns out, on closer inspection, to be related to the gaudy fairground decorations that Blake had studied since his student days. Certainly its battered surface is a far cry from the cold perfection of much abstract painting and has a similar used look to the images

above. The board gives the impression of being a found object, but possibly the artist has used his training as a commercial artist in painting the chevron pattern to make it resemble some ephemeral decoration.

The format of collaged elements of popular culture placed on top of a more abstract base was one that Blake used with great success in a number of works at this time. The subject of these collages or constructions included pop stars such as Elvis Presley, the Everley Brothers as well as pin ups and film stars. The artist's use of popular imagery clearly linked him to Pop Art but there are qualifications to be made, the most important is his attachment to a much wider definition of 'Pop' than the use in this work of five American pop stars would suggest. Blake brought his own personal emphasis to the incorporation of elements of popular culture. His works of this period neither function as an uncritical celebration of a bright vision of a modern consumer society nor as a cold analysis of the power of the media. Instead they frequently represent the consumer's view, the bedroom wall of the girl in the song or the collector or hoarder of pop ephemera. It is thus significant that when, a few years ago, the record was stolen from the painting, the artist was able to replace it with a second copy from his own collection.   GS

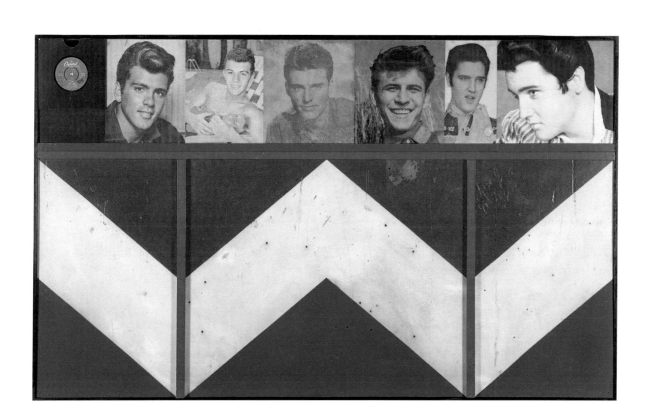

The Twin Towers of the Sfinx, State I 1962

Eduardo Paolozzi (b.1924) British

Gunmetal 1635 x 1350 x 610 mm

Purchased from the artist in 1964 (S.3.1964)

Much of the fascination of modern and contemporary sculpture lies in its making, in the variety of techniques adopted by sculptors intent on extending the traditional frontiers of sculpture.

Eduardo Paolozzi has, more than anyone, helped to develop the idea of collage, which was such a liberating influence for two-dimensional designers in the early days of the modern movement into a valid sculptural technique. In the 1950s this took the form of using wax as a support; into this, found objects could be pressed, which could then be cut up and recombined, just as in true collage, before being finally cast into bronze. In the years 1960-62, which Paolozzi spent teaching in Hamburg, the artist began to develop a new approach which has been dubbed 'industrial collage'. Paolozzi had always been interested in machines, sketching regularly in London's Science Museum, but now his visits to ship-breaking yards and heavy engineering works became more directly incorporated into his working methods.

The Twin Towers of the Sfinx, State I is typical of a large group of works produced from machine, or machine-like components in the period 1961-63 around the theme of the tower, either singly or twinned. The distinction is an important one. Paolozzi sought out ready-made machine parts which he could order from catalogues and engineering supply warehouses. In fact most of the components were not 'found' but actually produced in a foundry to the artist's own specifications. Paolozzi employed professionals to produce blueprints from his drawings and models, and these were then mass produced in the same way as any machine part.

Machine parts and pseudo machine components were then sent to a second firm where they were assembled by welders working from drawings sent by the sculptor from Germany. Initially the joins were only spot welded so that when Paolozzi returned changes could easily be made. The final joins were made by both welded seams and by bolts and were deliberately left rough to contrast with the high finish of the rest.

Looking at the works collectively one recognises time and again the same components; to use the analogy of language, Paolozzi first created the components/vocabulary, then assembled them to form different statements; though each was unique they were nonetheless governed by the same syntactical structure, namely the tower format. The rôle of the artist is thus more akin to the industrial designer in that his primary function is to formulate the idea and then to direct the labour of others in its execution. The end product, as in all industrial processes, is a collaboration of many efforts.

Though the process of making is interesting in itself, it does not answer the question of why? to what end so much effort? The title, *State I*, suggests the repetitive, sequential nature of the group; there is in fact a *State 2*, equally fullsquare and symmetrical. The word 'Sfinx' gives us another clue. The Sphinx in Greek legend was the inscrutable guardian of the riddle; at the same time the sphinx of the desert offers a formal equivalent to the solid, stocky quality of the towers. Like the Sphinx, the sculpture offers no solution or explanation of its existence, resolutely refusing to move or communicate. Looking at some of the other tower images Paolozzi produced at this time it is clear that the tower format symbolizes the faceless forces of officialdom weighing down upon the individual.

The work is full of fascinating contradictions; it is formed of two towers which refuse to soar or indicate height; it is a machine, made of machine parts, but does not move. Its very machineness is the product of artifice, the product of an artist who commands others to produce it. In fact Paolozzi also had a rather more literal meaning in mind. He called the towers "a kind of commentary on Germany"; "they remind me", he went on, "of German town halls, and the circular disk comes from a cutter the German housewife still uses to cut equal slices of cake."

GS

The Whitworth Tapestry 1967-8

Designed by Eduardo Paolozzi (b.1924) British

Woven at the Dovecot Studios, Edinburgh Tapestry Company
Wool and terylene tapestry on linen warps 2134 x 4267 mm
Purchased in 1968 with the aid of grants from the Arts Council of Great Britain
and the Friends of the Whitworth (T.12315)

The Whitworth Tapestry was commissioned by the Gallery to mark the official opening of the newly modernised galleries on 22 March 1968. It was woven under Archie Brennan at the Dovecot Studios of the Edinburgh Tapestry Company to a design by Eduardo Paolozzi, who waived his design fee.

Eduardo Paolozzi's collage design for the tapestry was based on a series of ten screenprints entitled *Universal Electronic Vacuum* (1967), which explored the artist's interests in popular culture and in computer technology. In the tapestry, the computerised figures of Walt Disney's Mickey and Minnie Mouse and Donald Duck, the strips resembling computer punch-card patterns, and the jewel-bright colours have great power to delight and amuse the viewer. As with the individual prints it is designed as a collection of heterogeneous images, lacking a single focal point.

The Edinburgh Tapestry Company was set up in 1912 by the Marquess of Bute, employing two master weavers trained at William Morris's tapestry workshop at Merton Abbey. The Dovecot Studios were, from the first, imbued with the principles of the Arts and Crafts Movement, particularly the belief that the weaver is a craftsperson who must be allowed a creative role in the execution of the work. The practice of imitating, in tapestry, work produced in another medium grew up in the nineteenth century and is still normal practice in many tapestry workshops today, for example, the state-run workshops at Aubusson in France. Precise colour-coding on the cartoon leaves the weaver with little to do but to translate each passage as precisely as possible; it is a sort of highly-skilled 'painting by numbers'. At the Dovecot Studios, however, an artist's design is never copied, but translated and interpreted, an altogether subtler and more difficult procedure. According to Archie Brennan, the resulting tapestry should be "a proper *extension* of the original work... such that the tapestry will have an identity that is its own".

Thus, the success of a reproductive tapestry depends almost entirely on the relationship between the designer and weaver, on the skill with which the weaver can translate an artist's work into textile form. It is a relationship fraught with danger, for whilst a musician may interpret a composer's music with impunity, the painter's work is usually considered taboo. *The Whitworth Tapestry* seems to have evolved freely through the close collaboration between Paolozzi and the weavers at the Dovecot. Creative decisions were made during the weaving with the artist's approval, and Paolozzi went on to design several further tapestries for the company.   JH

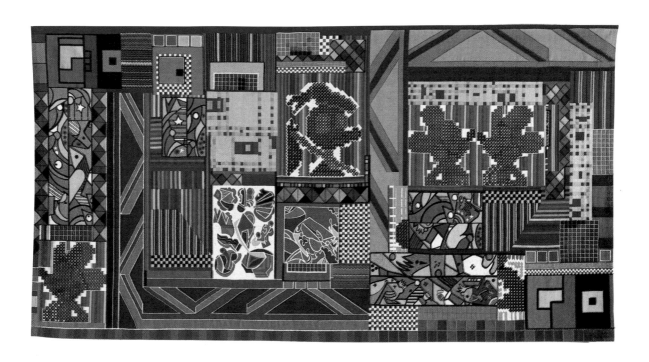

Peter Schlesinger 1967

David Hockney (b.1937) British

Pencil and coloured crayons 428 x 356 mm

Presented by the Friends of the Whitworth in 1968 (D.1.1968)

A modern collection, if it is to develop a lively character must support young artists. In the 1960s the Gallery was noticeably successful in this respect; it gave exhibitions to, and purchased works from, a number of artists who have since achieved international fame. The best known example was David Hockney; in 1969 the Whitworth organised his first exhibition in a British public gallery and by 1971 had also acquired two drawings. Although one tends to assume that oil paintings represent the more important side of an artist's work, in the case of Hockney, his ability as a draughtsman is such that the Gallery's decision to buy drawings, made partly on financial grounds, has proved to be fortuitous. In addition to the view, widely held amongst artists and critics, that Hockney's greatest strength lies in this area, there is also the undeniably attractive feeling that the drawings are more personal and deeply felt.

This latter point however raises a number of important questions about the relevance of personal biography to our appreciation of a work of art. A biographical approach to Hockney's work has not, however, in any way been discouraged by the artist himself. He has consistently produced portraits and life studies of friends and lovers and has allowed these to enter the public domain via his dealer. He has also written an autobiography which has provided all the necessary details to place his works firmly in such a context. Other artists may regularly portray close friends, but we are less likely to speculate about their relationship to the sitter. With Hockney however, and a subject like Peter Schlesinger, whom the artist portrayed in a long series of intimate studies over the course of four or five years, the facts of their relationship are so well known that they often intrude. Drawings of this private nature have traditionally only entered public galleries after the artist's death when curiosity about the artist's life is more acceptable.

This study of Peter Schlesinger was made in London in December 1967. The medium—coloured crayons, and the pose—a friend caught off guard, are typical of the studies of Peter and of the much larger group of informal sudies from life, which Hockney had begun in 1966. After a period in which his major preoccupation had been with a more stylized approach to problems of representation, the artist became more concerned to capture the appearance of life. "To me, moving to naturalism was a freedom. I thought, if I want to, I could paint a portrait;... I could do a drawing of someone, I could draw my mother from memory, I could even paint a strange little abstract picture...". Complaining in general terms that painters had made a mistake in, what he called, abdicating "to the camera", Hockney underlined the personal origins for his return to a more figurative based art. "The painting of people is too deep in us, everybody is interested in faces. To tell you about another person is a very deep thing in people and it's going to come out in some way or other."

Typically for this period the drawing was not produced as a study for a finished work or as a commission, nor was it produced directly for sale. The artist was thus free to develop only those areas that interested him. This, rather surprisingly, does not include the face, which is only partly worked in, and the hands. What makes this such an attractive drawing is the fascinating play between naturalistic detail and the more abstract, unfinished areas. This is a study where the aim is to understand the subject better and to develop technique and "not to bother what the reaction of the sitter was ... I'm not making the drawings for them, I'm making them for myself." Thus the importance of the very unselfconscious nature of these portrait drawings. Hockney has consistently sought out situations where capturing a likeness could occur where the subject had no opportunity to prepare a face. The subject caught unawares allows the artist and his relationship with the subject to come to the fore. Shorn of all biographical details it is still very clear that the starting point for this drawing, not least as a result of the very sensual handling of the medium, is the close personal involvement of the artist with his subject.　　　　　　　GS

Peter   Dec 67
67.1

Man's Head (Self Portrait 1) 1973

Lucian Freud (b.1922) British

Oil on canvas 533 x 508 mm

Purchased in 1977 with grants from the Victoria and Albert Museum
Purchase Grant Fund and the Friends of the Whitworth (O.1.1977)

Lucian Freud is one of a loosely knit group of painters, including Francis Bacon, Leon Kossoff, Frank Auerbach and Michael Andrews who have, for want of a better term, been called the School of London. In spite of differing attitudes and a strong sense of individuality there are enough links, in terms of friendship (Bacon's portrait of Freud is p.116) and in their unswerving commitment to the figure and to oil painting, to justify the label of a school, albeit with qualifications.

One distinction to be made between Bacon and Freud concerns the importance of the model. Bacon prefers to work from a photograph, or from memory, so as to liberate his imagination, whilst Freud believes that when painting from life you can "take liberties which the tyranny of memory would not allow". Freud is also more obviously grounded in the humanistic tradition of portraiture. For thirty years he has painted and repainted friends and colleagues in a narrow range of poses all resolutely studio bound; "who else can I hope to portray with any degree of profundity?" he has asked. If Freud has set himself a limited task it is nonetheless a dauntingly difficult one for such an honest and exacting artist. "I would wish my portraits to be of the people, not like them...", he has said. "I didn't want to get just a likeness like a mimic, but to portray them, like an actor... the paint is the person. I want it to work for me just as flesh does."

Freud has painted himself on more occasions than perhaps any contemporary painter. If brought together from every period of his career, these self portraits would represent a unique record of physical change and of stylistic development. This particular example is one of a group painted on a smallish scale in 1973. One of the most distinctive features of Freud's self portraits is that the artist freely admits the presence of the mirror, sometimes including it in the work itself, but always making it clear to the viewer that the object of the subject's intense gaze is himself. Most of them concentrate just on the head, occasionally including the shoulders; and in only one is there any indication of the activity of painting. It is as though the business of art can be simply reduced to the act of looking. The concentration on the head and one hand, caught in isolation and viewed close up, coupled with the stark artificial lighting, underline the intensity of the commitment required. The pose and the lighting combine to suggest a sense of unease and tension which verges on the self-conscious and the dramatic.

Given the traditional reading of a self portrait in terms of its capacity for self revelation, and knowing something of the artist's family background (born in Berlin, the grandson of Sigmund Freud) it is tempting to read too much into Freud's portraits of himself. Portraits can convince us that we know the subject, not because they impart some new information or magically reveal some hidden depth, but because they suggest a physical presence and thus engage a process of sympathetic recreation. In this case the low viewpoint and the intense artificial light throw into relief the hollows and protruberances of the face and these are caught and recreated by the swirling rich impasto of the pigment. The very tangible, physical quality of the paint can thus persuade us of the fiction that 'the paint is the person'. But what Freud means by this term is not a simple reading of character from physiognomic likeness but the seeking and attainment of a translation of form into another language, that of painting.　　　　GS

Interior at Oakwood Court 1978-83

Howard Hodgkin (b.1932) British

Oil on panel 813 x 1372 mm

Purchased in 1983 with grants from the Victoria and Albert Museum
Purchase Grant Fund and the Friends of the Whitworth (O.9.1983)

Artists have no binding duty to explain the meaning of their works and the viewer must often be patient before a complex and initially difficult work. Often one must work hard to find an explanation through a detailed study of the work, its antecedents or historical and artistic context. Conversely one can choose to surrender oneself to the more obvious attractions of colour and pattern and let the meaning take care of itself, springing independently from one's own experience.

If we are to pursue the first approach the best place to begin is with the title: *Interior at Oakwood Court*. We are invited, in view of the quite specific information given, to resolve some of the shapes and colours into elements of an interior. The effect of the band of red framing the picture, coupled with the patch of green in the centre, is to give an indication of recession, of a constructed space. At the same time, the rich surface pattern denies this and the thick impasto of pigment reminds us of the two dimensional reality of the work. The horizontal format is actually more suggestive of a landscape but the colouring again contradicts this, it is too synthetic, too rich.

If we turn to documentary evidence we are on more solid ground. The artist, in a letter to the Gallery, has said that "it is simply a portrait of two friends in their apartment in Oakwood Court". Whether we can read any of the shapes as two figures or not is perhaps irrelevant, compared with the confirmation of one's suspicion that the gloriously rich coloration of the work is a metaphor for the close personal involvement of the artist with his subject matter. These colours are emotional, warm in the most human sense. But "a portrait of two friends"? To understand this requires more information about the artist's approach to painting.

In looking for help with a work of art, statements made by the artist can be invaluable. Hodgkin is by nature a reticent man but nonetheless has made a number of useful comments. "When they're portraits of people" he has said "they would be an accumulation of experiences of that person". In other words, this is a portrait in which the artist is not so much concerned with likeness as with his own engagement with a subject, in this case two people, over a long period of time. Hodgkin has also said that "most of my works have nine, ten, twelve lives" and close inspection of the wooden panel on which our picture is painted shows that it has been worked over on a number of occasions in the five or so years that it took the artist to complete the work. Clearly a work showing two friends in an interior, painted and repainted over a period of time, is also an exercise in memory, of recapturing a look, a feeling or an emotion, as well as a summing up of accumulated personal experience.

A successful work (or one that is finished in Hodgkin's terms) must accomplish still more than this. It must also transform "the original feeling, emotion, or whatever you like to call it into an autonomous pictorial object" something which is a "harmonious impersonal structure". A public work of art is a strange place to work over personal feelings and for a very private person such as Hodgkin this requires what he calls a "sort of evasiveness of reality". What this means in practice is that the luminous colour must indicate two things: an emotional commitment by the artist to his subject matter, and an essentially impersonal, decorative language for the viewer. The artist is thus both confessional and private, tantalizing and enigmatic. He must make the viewer feel that the effort spent in unravelling the mystery of the work is reward enough, even if the problem is never resolved; in this the seductive quality of the colour is fundamental in keeping the viewer involved in the search.　　GS

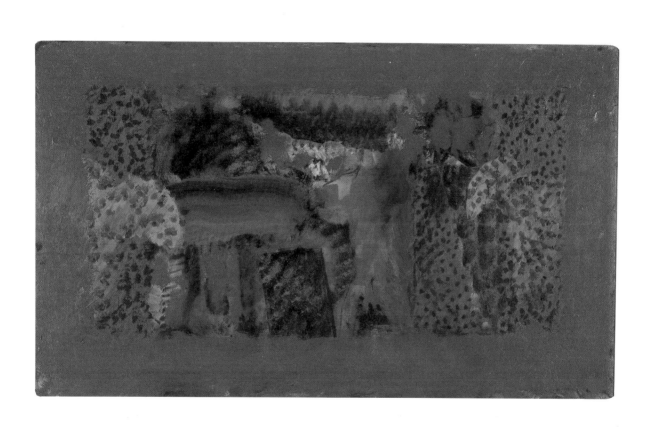

Côte d'Azure 1982

Designed by Collier Campbell Limited British

Manufactured by Christian Fischbacher (FISBA) Limited
as part of the Six Views collection
Screen-printed cotton furnishing fabric 4000 x 1420 mm (Repeat size: 920 mm)
Presented by the designers in 1987 (T.6.1987)

A degree of inevitable risk is involved in collecting contemporary art and design. What appears today to be new and exciting may well, with the benefit of hindsight, prove not to have had any lasting influence or significance, and end up as a 'white elephant' in the museum's or gallery's store. This is most unlikely to be the fate of Susan Collier and Sarah Campbell's design work. They have already emerged as one of the most innovative design teams of the 1980s, and their *Six Views* collection has been a resounding commercial success. In 1984 it won both a Design Council Award and the Duke of Edinburgh's Award for outstanding achievement in design. *Côte d'Azure* is probably the most popular design from the collection.

The design evokes the atmosphere and skyline of the South of France, and has a painterly feel which is characteristic of Collier Campbell's work. All of their designs, whether floral, abstract or inspired by the techniques and colours of ethnographical textiles, begin life as paintings and many retain in their final version the effect of brushstrokes. It is this quality, together with their strong designs and rich colour schemes, which makes their work instantly recognisable wherever it is sold under licence, be it Habitat, Liberty's or Martex, the American manufacturer of bed linen.

Collier Campbell Ltd was formed in 1979 by the sisters Susan Collier and Sarah Campbell after working together for more than a decade producing best-selling designs to the textile industry. They license designs to textile manufacturers and retail outlets, and have also expanded into other product areas such as bed linen, stationery and travel goods. The *Six Views* collection was licensed to the Swiss-based company Christian Fischbacher for sale in the United Kingdom, Europe and Japan. All six designs are produced in several different colourways.

Collier Campbell's furnishing fabrics sell well in both the contract and domestic markets, but their vibrant and accessible modern designs work especially well in intimate rooms in which objects are cluttered for their associative qualities rather than displayed as trophies of culture.

JH

Lloyds 1986

Designed by Brendan Neiland (b.1941) British

Printed by Brad Faine at Coriander Studios, London; published by Coriander Studios and Brendan Neiland
Screenprint, printed in colours; image size 762 x 508 mm

Purchased in 1987 (22,486)

The 'Lloyds', referred to in the title of this screenprint, is the recently completed building designed by Richard Rogers and Partners as the London headquarters of Lloyds Insurance Brokers in Lime Street.

The print shows two buildings' surfaces, one directly, and one as a reflection. The shining, repeated semi-circular forms contain the escape staircases, and are part of one of the six towers housing lifts, stairs, washrooms and service ducts, which stand outside the main fabric of the Lloyds building. The staircases have a bright aluminium cladding, a striking textural contrast to the smooth matt finish of the concrete tubular members which span other parts of the building; the gleam of these repeated aluminium shapes, visible above the skyline from some distance away, is one of the most exciting and attractive qualities of the building.

Both Richard Rogers and Brendan Neiland are known for their concern for, and fascination with, the urban environment. Rogers has written that one of his aims in designing the Lloyds building was to "link and weave together" the large 1960s office blocks nearby with the more complex and richly decorated smaller Victorian buildings of the city. For Neiland, however, it is the way in which the building stands out from its surroundings that makes it so exciting and attractive. Neiland has for many years been making prints and paintings from studies of modern office blocks in urban settings, but the first sight of the new Lloyds building must have come as a shock. "By chance, two years ago", he writes, "as I was strolling through the Bank and City areas of London with my youngest daughter, we were both staggered by a series of rippling, weaving and tubular reflections. Such a contrast to the ordered structure of so many buildings. How well they looked in the severer containing structures. They had to form the basis of a series of paintings and the print *Lloyds*."

Neiland has tended to make prints and paintings in similar ways, using spray guns and stencils for both media, though working on a much larger scale in his paintings than his prints. The most important part of this process is always Neiland's analysis of the image in terms of the separate colours which are built up layer upon layer. The success of the image depends to a great extent on his knowledge of how to manage such complex layering, and on his full understanding of all the subtleties of tone that can be created by the careful use of a spray gun. The actual production of this print was very much a joint effort between Neiland himself and Brad Faine, the printer at Coriander Studios with whom he has worked for over ten years. Following initial discussions with Faine about the image, the size of the print, the paper to be used and, above all, the likely number of colours to be printed, Neiland spent some weeks in his studio in France working on drawings and stencils for the print. He then handed the materials over to Faine, who worked on and developed the print and its coloured layers until he had produced a working proof of the final image. From this point, artist and printer worked together, changing the colours, their density, the order in which the screens were to be printed, and adding more screens until finally Neiland was satisfied with the result.

The final image is reminiscent of the way in which the world appears through the lens of a camera. Often in the past Neiland has studied the way in which a shiny, glass-fronted office building seems almost to dematerialize as the lens of a camera (or for that matter our eyes) focuses on a passing cloud reflected in its surface. In the *Lloyds* print, however, one surface remains firm, its linear structure undistorted, whilst one of the building's most striking aspects, the shining staircase, seems to float and bend, distorted like a mirage before us. This view of the building is quite understandable to anyone who has come upon it unexpectedly whilst walking through the City of London.   SH

British Drawings and Watercolours

The Whitworth's collection of British drawings and watercolours dates from the time of the Gallery's foundation, when a grant from the Guarantors of the Royal Jubilee Exhibition held in 1887 enabled the Institute to purchase a number of important English watercolours, including works by J.R Cozens, Turner, De Wint, Samuel Prout, and William Henry Hunt. Another early gift was Turner's watercolour of *The Chapter House, Salisbury Cathedral* (p.62), presented by William Agnew, one-time President of the Council of the Gallery and head of the firm of Thomas Agnew and Sons. In addition, a handsome donation from John Edward Taylor, proprietor of *The Manchester Guardian*, a selection of 154 drawings from his own collection, was received by the Gallery between 1891 and 1893. This selection was described at the time as having been made "with a special regard to the aim of the Institute at developing the Exhibition of the History of Art of Watercolour painting in England".

William Blake's *Ancient of Days* (p.66), undoubtedly one of the Gallery's most celebrated works, along with six other Blake watercolours illustrating Milton's *Hymn on the Morning of Christ's Nativity* were part of Taylor's gift. Other highlights from Taylor's collection were Paul Sandby's *Ludlow Castle*, John Robert Cozens' *Lake Nemi looking towards Genzano* (p.58) and *Rome for the Villa Madama*, Rowlandson's *High Life* and *Low Life*, Edward Dayes' *Greenwich Hospital*, Constable's *Feering Church and Parsonage*, and Bonington's *Shipping off the French Coast*. The most remarkable aspect of this collection, however, is the large group of watercolours by Turner and Girtin. *Tattershall Castle*, *Durham Cathedral and Bridge* (p.60) and *The West Front of Peterborough Cathedral* were among his finest Girtin drawings, while his gift of Turner watercolours amounted to more than twenty examples, including the very early *East End of Canterbury Cathedral*, *Coniston Fells*, *Fire at Fennings Wharf*, and a lively impression of *Petworth Park*. The gift also included a number of drawings by some less well known artists of the period, for example *Bagnigge Wells* by John Sanders

and *Lions Disturbed* by Samuel Howitt. In 1895, Taylor made an additional gift of one hundred and twenty seven drawings by William Mulready.

Although the nucleus of the Whitworth's collection of British drawings and watercolours had been formed within the first five years of the Gallery's existence, it was soon to be enriched even further by Mrs James Worthington's bequest in 1904 of another important group of works. These included J.R. Cozens' *Valley of the Isarco near Brixen*, Samuel Prout's *The Market Place, Wurzburg*, and several fine Turner watercolours, including *The Porch of Malvern Abbey*, *River Landscape with Castle*, and three early views of Hampton Court in Herefordshire.

By this time, 1904, the development of watercolour painting in Britain between c.1750 and c.1850 was well represented in the Gallery's collection. In fact, the great authority on Turner, A.J. Finberg, writing in the London *Star* in 1905, selected the Whitworth as one of the three most important centres in the country where English watercolours could be studied to advantage, the other two being the British Museum and the Victoria and Albert Museum. Even so, there were serious gaps. The Gallery had no examples of the work of Alexander Cozens or Francis Towne, both of whom were to be re-evaluated a few years later by Paul Oppé, and only one watercolour by John Sell Cotman, *Wreckage in a Rough Sea*. The collection lacked works by Jonathan Skelton, "Warwick" Smith, John Ruskin, Samuel Palmer and Edward Lear, but these deficiencies were to be remedied in due course.

In 1906 A.E. Anderson presented *Harlech Castle* by John Varley to the Gallery and during the following thirty years his numerous gifts included works of the highest quality. It was this generous and perceptive benefactor who gave Thornhill's two views of the River Thames at Hampton Court, Cotman's *Study of Trees at Harrow*, J.R. Cozens' *Between Bolzano and Trent*, De Wint's *Landscape with Church Tower*, Gainsborough's *Classical Landscape* and *La Forêt, after Jacob van Ruisdael*, Palmer's *The Sailor's Return*, Romney's *Study for the Gower Children*,

Rowlandson's *Stud Farm* (p.54), and drawings by Constable, Cox, Farington and Ward.

Numerous other benefactors have helped to enrich the collection of watercolours over the years. Notable gifts or bequests came from members of the Allen family, including Turner's *A Conflagration, Lausanne* and *Sunset at Sea with Gurnets*. Sir Edward and Lady Tootal Broadhurst bequeathed a large group of drawings by David Cox, and Jesse Haworth important Pre-Raphaelite watercolours. J.R. Cozens' *Lake Albano* and Crome's *Houses and Wherries on the Wensum, Norwich* were among Sir Thomas D. Barlow's handsome gifts to the Whitworth, while, in more recent times, Margaret Pilkington was not only the most generous of donors but also a discriminating expert in the field, which meant that her gifts were chosen with scholarly care and sound aesthetic judgement. They included *Peamore Park* by Francis Towne, *The Ferry* by Francis Wheatley, and *The Galleria di Sopra, near Albano* by Richard Wilson.

Since the Whitworth became the Gallery of the University in 1958, every effort has been made to strengthen the watercolour collection and, among other accessions, it has been enriched by the addition of Skelton's *Canterbury Castle*, John Martin's *Manfred and the Witch of the Alps*, Ruskin's *Mer de Glace*, and Thomas Daniell's *Small Hindu Temple*. The Department's most important acquisition in this later period was undoubtedly the group of seven sketchbooks by John Robert Cozens. In these the artist recorded landscape views on his trip to Italy with William Beckford, 1782-83. The seven books contain one hundred and ninety-three sketches from nature, most of which have some grey wash added to the pencil outlines. Many of the pages are dated and inscribed with the name of the place depicted in the drawing, and the Gallery now owns eight of the watercolours by Cozens based on these sketches. Four of these were already in the Gallery's collection when the sketchbooks were purchased in 1975, but four others have been acquired since then, these being *From the Road Between Caserta and the Aqueduct, The Small Temple at Paestum, The Coast of Vietri from Salerno*, and *Cetara, a Fishing Town on the Gulf of Salerno*. The purchase of these books was made possible with financial help from the Victoria and Albert Museum's Purchase Grant Fund, the Greater Manchester Council, the Pilgrim Trust, the National Art-Collections Fund, the Friends of the Whitworth and various private benefactors. Some two years later the Gallery managed to raise from various sources the £41,000 necessary to buy the only known surviving sketchbook of Thomas Girtin, thereby keeping it in this country. The sketchbook had been purchased for the Yale Center for British Art at Sotheby's in July, 1977, but the Reviewing Committee on the Export of Works of Art withheld an export licence for three months. Contributions toward the sketchbook's purchase for the Whitworth included a donation from the artist's great-great-grandson, Mr Tom Girtin, and his wife. The book contains three attractive watercolour compositions, a pen and ink portrait sketch of the artist John Raphael Smith, and nineteen pencil studies of seascape and landscape subjects, including views of Battersea Reach, Bolton Abbey and Harewood House.

The Whitworth has acquired two large collections of British drawings since 1958. The first, formed by Charles Sewter for the History of Art Department, was transferred in 1960, and the second was the Hector J. Towlson bequest received in 1970. Among the more important items from the History of Art Department's collection were a volume of landscape studies by Thomas Sunderland and interesting groups of drawings by Sir Edward Burne-Jones and W.R. Sickert. The Towlson collection contained over seventy British drawings of the eighteenth and nineteenth centuries, including works by Robert Adam, Anthony Devis, John Glover, Thomas Hearne, J.F. Lewis and Francis Wheatley.

The collection as it now stands is particularly strong in eighteenth- and nineteenth-century landscape drawings, with a good representation of most of the leading masters like Wilson, Alexander and John Robert Cozens,

Gainsborough, Paul Sandby, Dayes, Turner, Girtin, Constable, David Cox, De Wint, Palmer and Lear. Turner, in fact, can be seen in all stages of his development, from youthful topographical compositions such as *Warwick Castle and Bridge* to the highly romantic visions of his late style. The work of the Pre-Raphaelites and their associates is well covered, with important series of drawings by Ford Madox Brown and Burne-Jones, and a group of four Holy Land scenes by Holman Hunt. Also well represented are the nineteenth-century artists who travelled widely around the Mediterranean countries and to North Africa or parts of Asia, among them George Chinnery,

Lear, William Muller and David Roberts. The collection admittedly has its weak spots, but it continues to be enlarged, and recent additions have included two Near Eastern drawings by J.F. Lewis, a Turner watercolour of *Great Malvern Abbey* and *Gatehouse, Worcestershire, from the North West,* Grand Tour subjects by William Marlow and William Evans, and *Yanwath Hall, Cumbria* by George Price Boyce. In this way, the good example set by John Edward Taylor and William Agnew in the early years of the Whitworth's history is still being upheld.

Francis Hawcroft

The Modern Collection

Surprising though it may seem, both the Van Gogh drawing of the *Fortifications of Paris* (p.94) and the G.F. Watts oil, *Love and Death* (p.92) were both finished in the same year, 1887. Whilst we might be tempted to call the Van Gogh modern, even though is is is as old as the Gallery, the Watts seems the product of a different age. In the interests of simplicity the following account concentrates on oils, works of art on paper and sculpture that have been produced in the course of the Gallery's history, regardless of whether they are modern in style or not.

The one exception to this all inclusive definition are those foreign drawings which, though they are earlier in date than 1887, prefigure later works that we happily define as modern. These encompass an interesting group of drawings by French artists of the mid-nineteenth century, including works by Millet, Breton, Daumier and Bastien-Lepage; there are also works by Mauve and his contemporaries in Holland. But it is the French drawings of the latter part of the nineteenth century that are the strongest. Most of these entered the collection in the interwar years, frequently as gifts from A. E. Anderson, Sir Michael Sadler and Sir Thomas Barlow. The collection was enriched in this way by drawings by Fantin-Latour, Puvis de Chavannes, Seurat, Signac, Boudin, as well as Van Gogh's *Fortifications of Paris,* a late Cézanne watercolour, *Study of Trees,* and a pastel portrait by Degas. The group of drawings by Camille Pissarro includes a number presented by the family.

Because the twentieth-century foreign works are small in number they are too rarely seen. Those who do not know the Gallery well may be surprised to learn that, in addition to the fine Blue Period watercolour, *Poverty* (p.98), the Gallery also has two other Picasso drawings. More surprising is the remarkable triptych by de Chirico, *The Philosopher.* Works by Munch, Klee, Vasarely, Vuillard and Matisse were adventurous acquisitions in the 1930s for a small regional gallery.

The British works of art in the Modern Collection are more representative and, taken with prints, give a com-

prehensive picture of all the leading movements of the century. These include at least one work, and sometimes a sizeable group, by most of the major artists. There are, of course, gaps and many of these are attributable to an early policy decision, made on financial grounds, to concentrate on works of art on paper. Sadly it has not always been possible to fill these gaps, but a number of oils, recently purchased or acquired by gift, go a long way to making up for earlier lost opportunities.

There are two ways of telling the story of the modern collection: in terms of a chronological account of its history, or by detailing the collection's strengths, by period, by style or by individual. The following is a mixture, since those who might wish to find out more about the precise order of accessions can turn to the Gallery's Annual Reports which give more specific information.

The temptation to begin such an account with Walter Richard Sickert is great. The Gallery has an oil of *The Church of Saint Jacques, Dieppe,* as well as watercolours and drawings from throughout his career. Of particular note is *The Horses of Saint Mark's* and a group of portrait sketches of Cicely Hey bequeathed to the Gallery by the sitter herself in 1980. More recently the Gallery has bought two oils by fellow members of the Camden Town Group, a view of *Houghton Place* by Spencer Gore and *Nude on a Bed* by Harold Gilman.

Whilst the Gallery holds a number of very conservative works produced well into the twentieth century by artists whose styles were formed a half century before, it is those artists who have something new to say that naturally stand out. A group of watercolour sketches, reminiscent of late Turner, by Wilson Steer represent a bold challenge to a tradition that, in the early years of the Gallery's history, had seemed to have played itself out. A renewed emphasis on drawing, shorn of its cold academic associations, was the hallmark of the group centered around the Slade School. The Gallery's collection of drawings by Gwen and Augustus John and their contemporaries including Lamb, McEvoy, Innes and Conder, as well as their teacher

Henry Tonks now seems, in the light of a renewed interest in figurative drawing, less a legacy of a provincial past and more a welcome evidence of a traditional strength.

Although we are beginning to rethink the traditional story-line of modern art, with its emphasis placed firmly on those individuals who most thoroughly absorbed the influence of the major modern movements, such as Post-Impressionism, Cubism, Futurism, Surrealism and Abstraction, it is still tempting to single out those who so courageously went against the mainstream. An early abstract oil by David Bomberg, bought in 1981, as well as drawings by William Roberts, Wyndham Lewis and Edward Wadsworth are from an exciting period when British art began to rise to the new challenges posed by artists on the Continent.

The Gallery, rather surprisingly, holds few works by artists associated with the Bloomsbury Group, but in general has a good spread of material for the interwar years. Three artists stand out in terms of the number and quality of their works in the collection. Stanley Spencer's important oil *Soldiers Washing* is complemented by a group of drawings including a commissioned portrait of Margaret Pilkington. The drawings by Paul Nash make up a remarkable series and again the Gallery has more recently been able to add a fine oil, *The Whiteleaf Cross*, to the collection. David Jones is similar in many ways to both Nash and Spencer, working quietly in his own idiom and producing drawings of the highest quality. It is with artists like Nash and Jones that one can best appreciate the sense of continuity that exists, in spite of all that the term 'modern' might imply to the contrary.

Sculpture was not entirely ignored and the Gallery acquired by gift from A.E.Anderson (who was as generous to the modern collection as in other areas) three bronzes by Jacob Epstein. Just as interesting are drawings by noted sculptors such as Frank Dobson and Eric Gill and the very early acquisition of a wonderful group of drawings by Henry Moore, the earliest of which predated his first one-man exhibition in 1928.

The Whitworth did not acquire its first abstract painting, Alan Davie's *Elephant's Eyeful*, until 1960 and the period since has seen a number of acquisitions that have served to redress an imbalance undoubtedly caused by a rather conservative approach in the past. The John Piper *Abstract Construction* of 1935 filled one such gap, as did the purchase of a tempera painting by Edward Wadsworth and a drawing, *John Deth*, by Edward Burra (p.108) which greatly strengthened the Gallery's holdings of work influenced by Surrealism.

Two drawings by Henry Moore, showing coal miners at work (p.112), were presented to the Gallery in 1947 by the War Artists' Advisory Committee, along with an oil painting and twenty drawings by other War Artists such as Paul Nash, Graham Sutherland, John Piper, Eric Ravilious, Anthony Gross, Edward Ardizzone and Edward Bawden. The size, diversity and quality of this gift acted as an important spur to the Gallery's acquisition policy.

In order to represent the diverse trends in post-war British art, the Whitworth— especially since the transference of the Gallery to the University—broadened its acquisition policy and tapped a number of new sources for support. The challenge of creating a collection that could truly represent contemporary art for a young student audience was one that was eagerly taken up. Equally important, and no doubt an added incentive was the modernisation programme. The new spaces formed by the architect John Bickerdike created a truly sympathetic environment for the display of modern art.

In the pursuit of this policy the Gallery received generous support from many quarters. The bequests of Margaret and Dorothy Pilkington included an oil by Ben Nicholson, *A Window in Cornwall*. Perhaps more significant was the recent Hal Burton bequest which included major works by Hitchens, Sutherland, Moore, Matthew Smith, Ceri Richards, Paul Nash and many others. The importance of such a bequest lies not so much in the names of the artists represented, though that is important, as in the sense of enthusiasm with which they were collected. This can act as an important balance to the inevitably institutional nature of all public collecting. With limited funds one feels bound to try and buy a little of everything, and this can lead to a sense of sameness amongst galleries, who can usually only afford one example of an artist's work.

Artists have also given the Gallery generous support allowing it to buy work at advantageous prices; this was particularly true of Howard Hodgkin (p.130) and Anthony Caro whose work was bought at the height of their international fame and when prices would have normally been beyond the Gallery's means. Others have made outright gifts—for example, in 1975 and 1977 respectively, L.S. Lowry gave *Industrial Scene* (to the Director's Appeal) and Victor Pasmore, *Architectural Relief Construction*.

When the Whitworth became part of the University, the History of Art Department transferred its teaching collection of prints and drawings to the Gallery, and this included works by modern British artists. In 1960, the Friends of the Whitworth presented a number of works including examples by Keith Vaughan, Bryan Wynter, Eduardo Paolozzi and Frank Auerbach and they have continued their support, helping with a number of major purchases including the Francis Bacon, and the Howard Hodgkin. Another source of help has been charitable trusts, in particular the Calouste Gulbenkian and the Granada Foundations. Their financial support has helped with the purchase of works by Peter Lanyon, David Hockney, Patrick Caulfield and many others.

The role of the Contemporary Art Society has also been important. The system by which subscribing galleries are periodically allocated works of art given to, or purchased by, the society has resulted in some outstanding acquisitions including works by John Walker, Michael Sandle and Roger Hilton.

If the sources for supplementing the Gallery's meagre purchasing funds are varied then so too are the reasons for acquiring works. One might have a particular space in mind, such as the large South Gallery which only the works of a few artists, including Gilbert and George, can adequately fill. More often than not space is a constraint, in particular with sculpture. The pieces by Hepworth, Moore, Chadwick and Frink, which were mainly acquired in the 1960s (the first two at specially reduced prices), are basically small in scale.

One also has to keep in mind a sense of balance: between the demands of the historical collection and the need to support contemporary artists; between abstract and figurative art; and even between one sort of abstraction, free and painterly, and another, more measured and mathematical in its origins. A work can be purchased as an example of a particular artist's development or in order to strengthen the Gallery's holdings of a period or a movement, or more commonly both.

The collection is particularly strong in works from the 1960s, a period that was fragmented into a number of different movements. Examples of Pop Art include Eduardo Paolozzi's *Twin Towers* (p.122), Derek Boshier's *Megaloxenophobia* and Peter Blake's archetypal "Pop" painting *Got a Girl* (p.120) along with other works by Richard Hamilton, Patrick Caulfield, R.B.Kitaj, David Oxtoby, Patrick Procktor and Colin Self. The Modern Collection also contains two pieces of Kinetic art: *Mobile* by Alan Dudley and *I.M.O.O.S* (Images moving out onto Space) by Bryan Wynter. Abstract works from the period include a number of Op Art works by Bridget Riley and her contemporaries, as well as constructions by Anthony Hill and Richard Lin.

The challenge of a modern collection is always to keep up to date and, if possible to anticipate: to buy good artists before they become expensive. There are dangers in this. Many an artist is inflated beyond all proportion by dealers and by publicity: many a change in taste turns out to be no more than a passing fad. But though mistakes can be made the risks are worthwhile for the contemporary collection of a Gallery is an infallible guide to its vitality and commitment to the future.   Greg Smith

The Print Collection

Of all the Gallery's departments, the print collection seems the subject of most confusion. Many visitors either express surprise that a gallery should collect 'prints' rather than 'originals', or admit that they are not sure exactly what is meant by the word 'print'. The aim of this introduction is, therefore, to answer some of the questions most frequently asked about the Whitworth's print collection.

The main question, 'what is a print?', is surprisingly difficult to answer. The word 'print' has a confusingly wide range of meanings—the typeset words in a newspaper, handwriting in capital letters, a child's picture printed from a cut potato, a photograph, or a sophisticated and expensive multi-colour reproduction of an oil painting. In the context of an art gallery, the word might be expected to refer to printed pictures, but by no means all types of printed picture are collected at the Whitworth. The truth is that the items in the print collection do not fit neatly into one easily definable category, and even amongst curators there is disagreement about which types of printed picture are worth collecting, and which are not. However, at least some of the confusion can be cleared up by looking briefly at part of the history of printed pictures.

Postage stamps, newspaper photographs and Rembrandt etchings are all printed pictures: that is, they are all images produced from a surface prepared with a design that can repeatedly be transferred to another surface, producing many identical images. Only the last of this list of items is currently collected at the Whitworth. In practice, art galleries have tended to concentrate on pictures printed by woodcut, engraving or lithography or by processes derived from these methods. Before the development of photography in the early nineteenth century, these were the only known processes for producing printed images. They were used to print pictures which conveyed information about a wide variety of things. Nonetheless, as people began to collect printed images, they began to look on some types as being more valuable than others, and a convention developed of dividing printed pictures into two categories: 'reproductive' prints and 'original' prints. The first category included prints which were made by one person (or one group of people) to reproduce images originally conceived in another medium by another person; this commonly meant that an engraving or woodcut would reproduce the appearance of an oil painting, in order to make a large number of much cheaper versions of the more exclusive and expensive image. The second category included images which were initially designed to appear as prints rather than being first designed in another medium. The work of designing and of cutting the plate was done by one person, often referred to as a 'peintre-graveur' (painter-engraver) because he or she was often primarily trained as a painter, and not in what was regarded as the more lowly craft of printmaking. The distinction between the two categories rests on the higher value accorded to the work of conceiving or inventing the pictorial image. An engraver making an 'original' print both invented and executed the image. Many collectors would only include the second type of print in their collection, although both types are owned by the Whitworth.

After the development of photography during the early nineteenth century, printmaking was never to be the same again. Photographic techniques could easily and cheaply perform the function of reproductive prints, although this very efficiency encouraged people to become dismissive of any printmaking technique in which photography was involved; photomechanical techniques were considered cold and impersonal and more value began to be placed instead on techniques in which the personal gesture of an artist working on to the printing plate was clearly visible. Once again two opposing categories of print developed; the 'photomechanical' and the 'original' or artists' print. Since artists' prints were time consuming and expensive to produce, new marketing techniques were introduced to encourage sales, such as the 'limited edition',—artificially keeping the prints produced down to a small number—or adding the artist's signature to many of the collections on which the Whitworth's print department is based were formed when the prejudice against photomechnical processes was at its height, few examples of this category of print are included in the Gallery's collection.

During the 1950s and 1960s, however, even the distinction between 'photomechanical' and 'original' began to break down, as artists began to use elements of photographic printing in their work. Nonetheless, a distinction remained between the use of photomechnical processes to reproduce another work, such as an oil painting by Lowry, and the use of the same processes to produce a newly invented image, designed solely to exploit the characteristics of certain printmaking processes: in the end, the intention of the person producing the print is the only distinguishing feature. Many people are confused by the fact that artists such as Lowry have added their signature to good quality, photomechanically-printed reproductions of their oil paintings. Few art galleries collect this kind of 'signed print'; since the artist designed the image to appear in oil painting, Lowry's intention is better seen in the original oil painting than in the reproductive print.

We are perhaps now in a better position to answer the second question. 'Why does the gallery only collect certain types of print?'. We own examples of both 'reproductive' and 'original' prints produced before the advent of photography. Not only did reproductive engravers reach very high degrees of skill (see for example, Bernard Baron's engraved reproduction of one of William Hogarth's paintings on p.42), but such prints are historically important, since they were the main way in which knowledge about the work of much admired painters, such as Raphael or Rubens, could be spread across different countries. As to the second pair of categories, the gallery has tended to collect artists' prints, designed solely for production in the medium of print, and to exclude examples of prints photomechanically reproducing images conceived in another medium. This attitude becomes more and more difficult to defend as the function of printed images changes and develops; it could well be argued that currently the most influential and exciting printed images—music posters and record covers, advertising posters, photographs of all kind—are all things which are excluded by the Whitworth's collecting policy. The reasons for this are partly practical, enforced by financial considerations. Although advertising posters, for example, would be very cheap to purchase, the provision of storage space would be enormously expensive; conservation costs would be equally as high. However, our collecting policies are frequently reviewed and it is possible that a wider range of modern printed images will be collected in the future.

The next obvious question is just what do we collect? Apart from buying current examples of the work of artist-printmakers year by year, we also buy historical works. These are bought for a variety of different reasons. Often we try to add prints which relate to the landscape watercolours for which the Whitworth is well known. One of the earliest of the Gallery's purchases was a complete set of J.M.W. Turner's *Liber Studiorum*, bought in 1906. These prints were made partly by Turner, who etched the landscape subjects in outline, and partly by professional printmakers, who added mezzotint tone to the plates. We also own, and try to add to, a number of prints by, or after, British watercolour artists such as John Robert Cozens, Thomas Girtin, Paul Sandby, John Sell Cotman and Samuel Prout. We try to ensure that the Whitworth owns examples of all the major printmaking techniques; linocuts by Henri Matisse and Claude Flight have been bought recently as we had so few examples of the way in which that medium has been used. Since the collection is frequently used by school and college students, we try to make sure that we own works by those artists who appear on examination syllabuses; the recent purchase of a set of Goya's prints of bullfights, *La Tauromaquia*, meant that at last students could see works of this important printmaker in the Whitworth. For the better known artists, it is also desirable that we own examples of the widest possible range of their work. Until recently, although we owned a number of Rembrandt's etchings of figure subjects, we owned no examples of his treatment of landscapes. This was changed by the purchase of *Landscape: Cottage with Haybarn*. In general we try to add sensibly to the work which is already in the Whitworth to broaden out the existing collection of historical prints, and try to add interesting examples of current printmaking. We tend to limit modern purchases to British and American work, since we have neither the funds nor the storage space to collect examples from all over the world. As far as funding is concerned, many of the Gallery's most treasured prints could not have been purchased without grant aid. The National Art-Collections Fund has come to our aid when we wished to buy prints to which our purchase funds would not stretch, and we are regularly helped by the fund administered by the Victoria and Albert Museum on behalf of the Museums and Galleries Commission. The Friends of the Whitworth have also contributed frequently to major purchases, such as the prints by Goya and Rembrandt already mentioned.

When shown newly purchased prints, visitors frequently ask 'who chooses what the gallery buys?'. This is normally done by the Assistant Keeper in charge of the print collection in consultation with the Director. It is perhaps inevitable that the personal interests of the current curator will, to a greater or lesser extent, affect the selection, but as curators change, so the emphasis of the collecting policy changes, and this means that over the years, variety is maintained in the additions made to the collection. Margaret Pilkington, in her position as Honorary Director of the Gallery from 1936 until 1959, used her special interest in wood engraving to add a very impressive collection of work by such British engravers as Eric Gill, David Jones, Paul Nash and Gwen Raverat.

Our collection is largely based on donations and bequests from people who have built up their own print collections, with varying aims and interests, and have decided that a gallery shall have them for public use. One of the earliest of such gifts was made in 1910 by G.F. Cox, who owned a fine collection of eighteenth-century British colour prints. The most spectacular gift was probably that made by G.T. Clough in 1921. His collection of mostly Renaissance and seventeenth-century prints included examples of work by many of the most admired printmakers: Albrecht Dürer, Andrea Mantegna and Rembrandt van Rijn. Many of these prints are now of such rarity and importance that only the richest museums or private collectors would be able to buy them. The prints by Zoan Andrea, Dürer and Rembrandt illustrated in this guide (p.20,22,30) were all given by Clough. Other bequests included prints of quite a different nature: in 1926 William Sharp Ogden gave a group of British prints, including portraits and topographical images. His collection was built up around a nucleus inherited from an ancestor, the engraver William Sharp, which reflected the different collecting interests current in the eighteenth century. A collection made with yet another purpose, that of teaching students aspects of the history of art, was transferred to the Gallery in 1960 by the University's History of Art Department. The Japanese colour woodblock prints which the Gallery owns were also mainly the result of gifts or bequests: in 1934 Mrs Max Meyer gave a group in memory of Professor Meyer, followed by gifts from Mrs O. Beer in 1931, and Joseph Knight in 1951. Not all gifts have been of large groups of prints; equally treasured are presentations of single prints such as Picasso's etching *The Frugal Repast* given in 1922 by Sir Michael Sadler.

It is difficult to answer the question 'what is in the collection?' without resorting to a list of names, which makes for very dull reading. Anyone who wishes to know what the collection contains is best advised to consult the current curator; an index of works arranged by the name of the printmaker is available in the Print Room for anyone wanting to know if we own work by a particular person. In brief, just over half the collection consists of work by

British printmakers. This includes a fine collection of the work of William Hogarth, as well as a group of seventeenth- and eighteenth-century landscape prints, and wood engravings of the 1920s and 1930s. The Italian school is the next largest, thanks mainly to the gift from G.T. Clough. This was based on work by wood cutters and line engravers of the sixteenth and seventeenth centuries, although we also own many prints by G.B. Piranesi. With the exception of Albrecht Dürer, we have relatively few works by German artists; the French School fares a little better, including some seventeenth-century portraits and a small number of prints by nineteenth-and twentieth-century painters such as Camille Pissarro, Paul Gauguin and Henri Matisse. Dutch and Flemish prints are small in number, and although we do own a number of etchings by Rembrandt, few are are equal in quality to the magnificent *Three Crosses* illustrated on p.30.

The final question which visitors often ask is 'what does the gallery *do* with these prints?' and, by implication, 'what use can we as visitors make of them?'. The most obvious use we make of the prints is to display groups of them in the Gallery, often focussing on a particular theme, or on a particular technique. This we hope will enable visitors to understand and enjoy looking at the rich variety of effects and images which printmakers can produce. We try to provide information about the prints in the form of labels or printed sheets, or by more practical demonstrations of printing which can occasionally be arranged. Since the print collection includes some 11,000 or more items, what is on display at any one time is clearly only the tip of the iceberg. The Whitworth is particularly fortunate in having a spacious and well-equipped Print Room, constructed in the mid 1970s in a previously unused first floor area of the Gallery. The majority of prints and watercolours not on show are stored here. The room can be used by appointment in much the same way as a reference library.

Finally, perhaps one of the collection's most exciting functions is to show that, like painting and drawing, artists need not have a monopoly on printmaking. Although the more complex printmaking techniques, such as etching or lithography, need expensive equipment, the more easily accessible and simpler methods such as linocutting or screenprinting can produce striking results. We hope that at least some of the Gallery's visitors will find in the collection not only a source of detached interest but a practical inspiration as well.

Sarah Hyde

The Textile Collection

Within the last hundred years the Whitworth has built up the largest and most comprehensive collection of flat textiles outside London, the range and importance of its holdings making it second only in importance to the collections at the Victoria and Albert Museum. Since one of the original intentions of Sir Joseph Whitworth's trustees had been to found a museum of the industrial arts in Whitworth Park, the development of this area of the Gallery's collections would surely have afforded them considerable satisfaction.

The textiles which were shown at the opening exhibition of the Whitworth Institute at Grove House in 1890 included a group of loans from the private collection of Sir John Charles Robinson (1824-1913), a noted Victorian collector and connoisseur who had been the first Superintendent of the collections at the South Kensington Museum (now the Victoria and Albert Museum) from 1852 to 1869. In that capacity he had travelled widely on the continent buying for the museum and for himself. The bulk of his purchases were made in Spain and in Italy, where many ecclesiastical vestments and other textiles came on to the art market in the late 1860s and early 1870s. In Italy a number of religious establishments were suppressed after unification in 1870, and a similar situation occurred in Spain during the civil disturbances which followed the deposition of Queen Isabella in 1868. Important items from these sources have since found their way into the collections of the Victoria and Albert Museum, the Royal Museum of Scotland and, of course, the Whitworth Art Gallery, for, in 1891, Robinson sold his entire collection of over 1000 textiles for the nominal sum of £3,750, thereby laying the foundations of the present collection.

The main focus of his collection was on European ecclesiastical material of the sixteenth to eighteenth centuries, and it includes altar frontals and hangings, altar linen, mitres, gloves, stoles, maniples, and embroidered orphreys from vestments. The most important pieces, however, are the vestments, amongst which are the mid-sixteenth-century Spanish funeral cope (p.24), a complete set of Spanish festival vestments of the seventeenth century, consisting of cope, chasuble, dalmatic, and tunicle, and a sixteenth-century Venetian cope of brocaded satin, its hood embroidered with Christ rising from the tomb. Sadly, many of the ecclesiastical embroideries require extensive conservation before they can be displayed, and the Gallery has so far been unable to establish a permanent post of textile conservator to enable this specialised work to be undertaken.

Robinson's collection was not confined exclusively to ecclesiastical material. There were also several hundred fragments of early silks, woven for secular as well as ecclesiastical use: damasks, brocatelles, brocades and velvets, again chiefly Spanish and Italian and dating from the fifteenth to the eighteenth centuries.

By 1891, when negotiations for the purchase of the Robinson collection had been completed, it had been significantly augmented by Sir Charles's recent purchase of over seventy Coptic fragments and garments and the rare, late fifteenth-century tapestry woven altar frontal from the Cologne region depicting the Tree of Jesse, one of the treasures of the Gallery's collection (p.18). Robinson's collection of Coptic textiles is associated with the renowned Victorian archaeologist Sir William Flinders Petrie, although it is not known which textiles derive from Petrie's own excavations and which from purchases he is known to have made whilst in Egypt.

The Whitworth's holdings in this area were strengthened considerably when the collection of Coptic textiles at the Manchester Museum was transferred to the Gallery on permanent loan in 1968. Of outstanding importance from this source are two exceptionally well-preserved embroidered panels of late fourth-century date depicting female portraits personifying *Autumn* (p.16) and *Winter*. The collection of Coptic textiles now numbers around 1000 pieces and is of international importance for the range of types and techniques which it embraces. It provides a complete record of the changes in design which took place in Egyptian textile manufacture between the period of the late Roman Empire and the early Middle Ages, when Egypt was ruled in turn from Rome, Byzantium, Damascus, and Baghdad. It includes several complete garments, examples of unusual techniques such as sprang and Coptic knitting, and early figured silks reflecting Islamic influence.

Apart from the Robinson collection, other textiles exhibited at the opening of Grove House in 1890 included three recently woven tapestries, *Flora* (p.86), *Pomona* and *Fox and Pheasants,* which were among the earliest products to come off the looms at William Morris's Merton Abbey workshops. They were shown at the Manchester Royal Jubilee exhibition in 1887 and soon after purchased for the new museum, showing great artistic judgement on the part of Whitworth's trustees. The textile collection now covers William Morris and the work of the other Arts and Crafts designers with considerable distinction. There are lengths of most of Morris's best known designs for printed and woven textiles, as well as a good selection of work by contemporaries such as C.F.A. Voysey, Lewis F. Day and Walter Crane. Many of the pieces were formerly in the textile collection of the Manchester Regional College of Art (now Manchester Polytechnic), which was transferred to the Gallery in 1966. Unique to the Whitworth is a series of pattern-books donated by Bernard Wardle and Co. Ltd. in 1962, which record the dye experiments carried out for Morris by Thomas Wardle between 1875 and 1883, before Morris set up his own printworks at Merton Abbey. British textile design of the nineteenth and twentieth centuries is in constant demand from students and teachers, and the department makes every effort to make its study collection easily accessible. Plans for an extension to the Gallery include the provision of a public area where a large number of these textiles will be available for study under glass.

There is reasonable coverage of most of the twentieth century, from a large group of Liberty Art Fabrics, produced c.1900, right up to the present day. Of special interest, given the unusual make-up of the collections at the Whitworth is an extremely good collection of artist-designed textiles. Dress and furnishing fabrics by Paul Nash, Henry Moore, John Piper, and Howard Hodgkin, amongst others, are matched by their work in other media in the Gallery. The emphasis is on industrially-produced textiles rather than on one-off craft pieces, although the department has made occasional purchases of tapestries, including a recent example by Marta Rogoyska (*Croce e Delizia,* 1982) and other wall-hangings. Again, the collection of twentieth-century textiles at the Whitworth is surpassed, in terms of range and quality, only by that at the Victoria and Albert Museum.

The Gallery led the way in this country in the early 1960s in beginning to systematically build up a collection of industrially-produced printed and woven furnishing fabrics, and for the post-war period it can now claim to be comprehensive. Purchases continue to be made on a regular basis, but the Gallery is also the recipient of many gifts from manufacturers. Warner & Sons Ltd regularly donate lengths from their contemporary design range, and other recent gifts have come from Designers' Guild and Collier Campbell Ltd. (p.132). The criterion for selection is innovative rather than just popular design, although care is taken to try to represent the broad trends in contemporary design. The department is firmly committed to the continued expansion of its contemporary holdings. Given that so few institutions have made this commitment to the systematic collecting of twentieth-century textile design, the Whitworth's collection will be of enormous future value to textile designers and historians.

In other areas, the collection of British textiles is weaker. The Gallery was founded at a period when the products of the local Lancashire cotton mills were not regarded as collectors' pieces, and, sadly, there is no permanent record, in terms of a textile collection, of the nineteenth-century Manchester cotton trade. Wherever possible, however, acquisitions of local interest are made, an example being the several hundred examples of printed cottons made in Manchester for export to Africa, India and Indonesia which were donated by the Calico Printers Association (CPA) in the 1960s.

British embroidery, one of the most popular areas of the collection with visitors to the Gallery, is also rather under-represented. Robinson's collection included Hannah Smith's casket (p.28), an early example of the small embroidered boxes or cabinets, the making of which became something of a craze in the second half of the seventeenth century, and there have been occasional later acquisitions of important items of early English domestic embroidery. These include the bodice from a lady's smock of the early seventeenth century, embroidered with naturalistic floral motifs characteristic of the Elizabethan and early Jacobean periods, a mirror with embroidered frame of 1660-75, bequeathed by G.F. Fox (1910), and a recently purchased crewelwork bed curtain of the late seventeenth century, embroidered with a 'Tree of Life' pattern. Fine professional embroidery is represented by a group of men's waistcoats of 1770-1800, formerly the property of Lord Stanley of Alderley and worn by one of his forebears. Garments such as these were reserved for court use and have thus been preserved in excellent condition. Otherwise, however, British embroidery is represented by relatively few distinguished examples of the craft.

The revival of lace making as a craft in the 1980s has brought with it a great deal of interest in the Gallery's collection of historical lace. This is an area of the textile collection which is still not fully appreciated but which is, in fact, of considerable distinction. It numbers around 1000 pieces and includes very good examples of rare sixteenth-and seventeenth-century Italian and Flemish laces, including gold and silver bobbin lace. The collection is a bit weak in the classsic Flemish and French laces of the eighteenth century, but there are good examples of nineteenth-century English, Irish, Maltese, and Flemish lace (p.74). Some of it was purchased from the collection of John Jacoby, a noted collector of and expert on lace, and a large group of several hundred pieces came from the Bock collection, previously owned by Manchester City Art Gallery, the College of Art and the Institute of Science and Technology.

In addition to its Coptic and modern collections, the Whitworth is particularly noted for its holdings of ethnographical textiles, the majority of which have only been acquired since the end of the Second World War. Foremost amongst these are some 400 pieces of Mediterranean and Islamic embroidery presented to the Gallery in 1949 by Professor and Mrs P.E. Newberry. The Greek and Turkish embroideries form the largest group and include outstanding examples of the large hangings, bed-curtains, hand-towels, and pillow covers (p.38) which girls embroidered as part of their dower chest. They date mainly from the seventeenth to the nineteenth centuries. Newberry's primary interest was in Egyptian textiles of the late Classical period, but his wife Essie, herself an accomplished embroideress, seems to have been the driving force behind the wide scope of what he called the 'modern decorative' textiles in the Newberry collection. It also includes a good group of embroideries from North Africa and Central Asia.

Again, the decision to transfer the textile holdings of the Manchester Museum to the Whitworth in the 1960s, when the Gallery had become part of the University, strengthened its own holdings of ethnographical material significantly and brought related material under one roof for storage and display. In the early 1970s a further step in the direction of this specialisation was made when the decision was taken to begin a collection of village rugs and other tribal material from Central Asia. This collection focuses primarily on the artefacts produced by the tribal groupings of the Türkmen and Qashqā'i of Iran, and includes a wide variety of material: rugs, saddle and storage bags, animal trappings, costume, and jewellery. The Whitworth material, together with a large group of loans, was shown in two major exhibitions mounted at the

Gallery in the 1970s, *The Turcoman of Iran* (1972) and *The Qashqā'i of Iran* (1976), and the colours and patterns of these textiles seem to be a source of constant inspiration to design students, who frequently study and draw from them. The changing lifestyle of the tribes, as they settle in the cities, and the political turmoil in the Middle East during the past decade mean that many of the traditions associated with the tribes are fast disappearing, making the Gallery an important centre for the study of their crafts.

This brief survey of the textile collection does no more than highlight its main areas of interest and distinction. It is well-known to teachers, designers and textile historians, who make good use of the material in the study collection. It is hoped that, by means of changing displays, temporary exhibitions and, perhaps, a new public study area, more non-specialists will also come to appreciate the full extent of its riches.

Jennifer Harris

The Wallpaper Collection

According to Lady Gregory, before expiring in the Hotel D'Alsace, Paris, in 1900, Oscar Wilde remarked "My wallpaper is killing me, one of us must go". Wallpapers, like textiles, are an integral part of most people's lives and, clearly, they have the capacity to soothe, delight, irritate or enrage. And yet they are amongst the most ephemeral of objects, subject to the ravages of time, war and changes in fashion. Thus, it is likely that many visitors would be surprised to discover that the Whitworth Art Gallery has a substantial collection of these ephemeral objects. It may be that the domestic surroundings of the majority of wallpapers with which we come into contact render them commonplace or apparently lacking in the distinction normally associated with 'works of art'. However, they have played an important part in the decoration of interiors in England since the sixteenth century and a study of the history of their design, production and marketing enables us not only to chart the main trends in interior decoration but also provides an indication of changes in social patterns and industrial prosperity.

Although the history of wallpaper in Britain can be traced back to the early sixteenth century, it was not until the late seventeenth century that printed papers began to compete with the traditional wallcoverings of the wealthy classes, such as tapestries, woven silks and decorated leather panels. Wallpapers were cheaper substitutes for such hangings although, initially, they faced competition from flocked canvas, which was not only more durable than printed or stencilled paper but, owing to its surface texture, was more reminiscent of woven textiles.

Early developments are well represented in the collection by late seventeenth-and early eighteenth-century Dutch, Flemish, and French embossed leather decorations (p.36), by fragments of English block printed and stencilled papers of the late eighteenth century (p.32), and the vogue for Chinese hand-painted decorations (p.52) and chinoiserie (p.50) is also exemplified. By the mid-eighteenth century the colouring and embossing of paper and the marketing of it had become "a Considerable Branch of Trade". In Britain the printing of the design by means of wood blocks and distemper colours was in use by this time and a number of other technological advances led to a rapid increase in the availability and popularity of printed papers.

All designs prior to 1830 were printed onto small sheets of paper which were pasted together, usually before printing, and this makes the production of the wide range of French scenic decorations produced for the luxury end of the market during the first quarter of the nineteenth century even more remarkable (p.64). Decorations such as these could take up to two years to complete but the development of continuous rolls of paper was the first of a number of advances which led to the mechanisation of the industry; by the middle of the nineteenth century, it enabled the rapid production of machine printed wallpaper, the very cheapest kinds of which sold for a farthing per yard. However, until the end of the century, papers printed by hand with pear wood blocks were regarded as being of the highest quality and it was by this method that the designs of William Morris were produced (p.78). The Whitworth's collection of Morris papers is extensive and, together with designs by other nineteenth-century figures such as A.N. Pugin, Owen Jones, Walter Crane, Lewis Day, and C.F.A. Voysey (p.102), it represents all the main artistic movements of the last quarter of the century.

By the turn of the century, the production of 'Art' wallpapers for the middle classes by firms such as Jeffrey & Co was being superseded by the mass production of cheaper decorations, and improvements in the printing, embossing, gilding and finishing of papers, together with various other mechanical refinements had enabled firms to diversify and cater for a market which looked for a wide variety of effects. 'Sanitary' papers which, with their smooth texture, lent themselves both to washing and varnishing, were popular until the First War, and papers which simulated glazed tiles, wood effects, relief decorations and the embossed leathers of the eighteenth century, were fashionable well into the twentieth century. Stencilling was re-introduced for the production of friezes and borders (p.100) and the popularity of this technique for cut-out decorations continued until the outbreak of the Second World War, when all wallpaper production ceased because of the lack of raw materials. The post-war period saw the development of a variety of new processes: screen printing, photogravure, flexographic and ink embossing. Public demand for greater durability was met by washable, ready-pasted wallcoverings, particularly vinyls, and these were more often textured than patterned. A series of papers and pattern books representing these developments was selected for the Gallery's first exhibition of wallpapers in 1972 and these were then added to the Collection.

The story of the Collection is itself an interesting one. The original impetus came from the desire of A.V. Sugden, one of the chairmen of The Wall Paper Manufacturers Ltd, to have records of the industry's achievements. This organisation, one of the industrial joint stock companies which were a feature of the last quarter of the nineteenth century, was established in 1899 and comprised many of the major English producers of wallcoverings. The Company's generous gift of its historic wallpapers to the Whitworth Art Gallery in 1967 resulted largely from the enthusiasm of Edward Pond of The Wall Paper Manufacturers in London, Robert Grime in Manchester, and Eric Entwisle, a former Director of the Company, who assembled a large part of the Collection between 1948 and 1967, and the transfer of the wallpapers to the Gallery marked a new phase in its acquisitions policy. Prior to 1984 new acquisitions of wallpapers were made on a rather *ad hoc* basis, usually by gift, and only when people came forward to offer material. Our Wallpaper Department does still indeed rely heavily on the generosity of donors, and we gratefully acknowledge our indebtedness to Edward Bawden for his recent gift of a selection of his wallpapers (p.104), and to Crown Wallcoverings Ltd. for their remarkably generous bequest of a large twentieth-century

collection (p.100), but we have also recently begun to purchase examples of historic wallpapers ourselves. Recent purchases include a rare example celebrating the French Revolution, a *trompe l'oeil* decoration, and a wallpaper frieze probably produced by Dufour et Cie c.1810, and purchased with the aid of a grant from the Museums and Galleries Commission/Victoria and Albert Museum Purchase Grant Fund.

The storage and care of historic wallpapers present unique problems, particularly if they had to be retrieved from damp and decaying environments, and for many years the collection was available only to specialist researchers. However, in 1984 with generous funding from the North Western Museum and Art Gallery Service, a Wallpaper Study Room was set up and grants from the British Academy and the Pilgrim Trust enabled us to pay for the cataloguing of the collection over a period of three years, which, in turn, meant that we could open up the collection. Since then, it has been the Gallery's policy to mount regular displays. These have included a range of Nursery Papers, a selection from the Arts & Crafts period, and a very popular display of William Morris wallpapers which, with the aid of a grant from the Greater Manchester Council travelled to Stalybridge and Bolton. These events culminated in the mounting of a major exhibition, *A Decorative Art*, in 1985, which attracted sponsorship from Crown Decorative Products, Osborne & Little plc, Marks & Spencer plc, and Colefax and Fowler Interior Design. This funding resulted in the receipt of a BSIS award under the new scheme set up by the Government to promote business sponsorship of the arts, and the exhibition generated considerable interest both among Gallery visitors and in the press and television.

The ephemeral nature of wallpaper is such that much of what survives is from the luxury end of the market. It either adorns the walls and ceilings of country houses or other grand interiors, or it survives in collections which concentrate on the lives and work of a few well-known designers. Inevitably, therefore, its historic study has generally been regarded as a specialist subject tending to focus on the evolution of styles and the rôle of the designer. However, recently it has become clear that a much larger audience is interested in wallpapers and the Whitworth's collection, encompassing as it does both the hand-painted and printed decorations of the wealthy, together with the cheaper machine printed papers intended for the popular market, is able to offer a broader view of the development of the wallpaper industry. The Department provides information and research facilities for scholars and others with special interests, and it organises guided tours for students of art and design and design history. It also gives advice and information on historic patterns to institutions and individuals involved in the refurbishing of historic houses.

The location of our collection in the North-West where the mechanisation of wallpaper production was pioneered seems to us to be particularly apposite and firms from the region have been remarkably generous. A grant over a period of years from Coloroll plc has enabled the essential programme of research and conservation to continue, and other links with industry are maintained by our own connections both with manufacturers who reproduce historic designs and with those whose current ranges are included in the twentieth-century collection.

The Wallpapers Department of the Whitworth Art Gallery has been at the forefront of the development of the recent new interest in the study of wallpapers, involving itself in the founding of the Wallpaper History Society and in an energetic exhibition and display programme. It is appropriate that the collection should be housed in an institution which was established to commemorate one of Manchester's most famous industrialists, and, as a centre for the study of wallpapers it is unparalleled outside London.   Christine Woods